WOMEN

*Beyond
Equal
Rights*

WOMEN

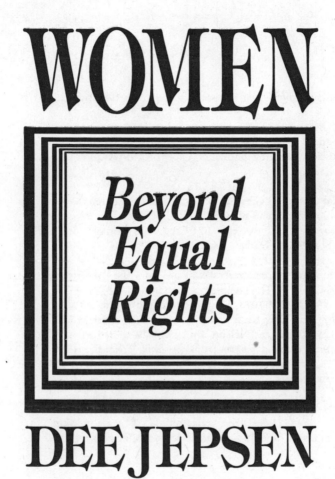

*Beyond
Equal
Rights*

DEE JEPSEN

WORD BOOKS
PUBLISHER
WACO, TEXAS

A DIVISION OF
WORD, INCORPORATED

Special thanks to Crescendo Corporation for extensive
quotations from the book BE SOMEBODY . . . by Mary
C. Crowley. © Copyright 1974 Crescendo Corporation
P.O. Box 28218, Dallas, TX 75228.

Scripture quotations marked NASB are from the *New American
Standard Bible,* © The Lockman Foundation, 1960, 1962, 1963,
1968, 1971, 1972, 1973. Scripture quotations marked NKJV
are from the New King James Version. Copyright © 1979,
1980, 1982, Thomas Nelson, Inc., Publishers. Scripture
quotations marked TLB are from *The Living Bible,* copyright
© 1971 by Tyndale House Publishers, Wheaton, IL. Used
by permission.

Quotations reprinted from *Her Name Is Woman, Book 1* by Gien
Karssen. © 1975 by The Navigators. Used by permission
of NavPress, Colorado Springs, Colorado. All rights reserved.

Library of Congress Cataloging in Publication Data:

Jepsen, Dee, 1934–
    Women: beyond equal rights.

    Bibliography: p.
    1. Women's rights—United States. 2. Feminism—United
States. 3. Women—Religious life. 4. Jepsen, Dee,
1934–   . I. Title.
HQ1426.J46 1984   305.4'0973   84–11854
ISBN 0–8499–0404–8

Printed in the United States of America

Dedicated to the women of our time—
women I have grown to
love sincerely and appreciate deeply,
whose value has yet to be realized

Contents

A Word of Gratitude

My first "thank you" goes to my husband, Roger, my biggest (and least objective) fan. I appreciate his encouragement and support for my writing this book, despite the fact this is a vulnerable year in his personal political career and the topic of women is politically sensitive and volatile these days.

Because of the short time available, completing this book has been an exercise in discipline, not only for me, but also for those who so ably assisted me. I realize that their faithfulness and commitment helped to make it all possible.

My debt of gratitude must also include the many women, and men, from whom I have gleaned words of wisdom, insight, and inspiration over the years, helping to bring into clearer focus my views of life and truth.

In addition, I am grateful for the confidence and good will exhibited by my publisher.

To you all, from my heart, a sincere "thank you."

Preface: Setting the Stage

I looked around the room that had become almost a second home to me for the last year. I wondered, for the first time, would I really miss it? And would I miss the job that had brought me here?

Many people would never think serving as a Special Assistant to the President of the United States could be simply a "job." Perhaps I should have been more impressed with the title. But as age fifty rapidly approached, nothing overly impressed me anymore. Years of living through good times and bad, successes and failures, had tempered my outlook.

How thankful I was for having found the special element that brought a stable perspective to my life. Being the wife of a United States senator or serving on the staff of a president could easily have overwhelmed me with pride or stifled me with intimidation. Except for fleeting times of human frailty, I had truly felt neither.

Now, nearly fourteen months later, the time had come to pass this task on to someone new and move into another role—campaign assistant and surrogate for my husband, Roger, as he began to seek reelection to the United States Senate. I had served with him on his election campaign in 1978 and as a personal unsalaried assistant in his Senate office for nearly four years, so working with him was nothing new to me. As Roger is so fond of saying, we are "a team."

As my eyes focused on my office in the Old Executive Office Building, I realized that not only would I miss the job, but also the wonderful friends with whom I had labored in the White House complex, and the place itself.

My office had become an expression of my personality and my tastes—dark blue rug, couch and chair, blue-and-white-checkered love seat, white drapes, light blue walls, touches of red in the accessories. Pictures, certificates, and plaques arranged on the walls made memories come alive. Visiting friends often said, "Dee, I would have known that this was your office even if no one had told me. It looks just like you."

Hanging above the bookcase was a painting I had done of Mother Teresa, a special heroine of mine. Its sepia shades contrasted sharply with the vivid colors I had used in the other paintings in the room, and seemed to give dramatic emphasis to the woman's totally unaffected approach to life. Holding an infant in her gnarled hands, she is gazing at the child through twinkling eyes set deep in her wrinkled, smiling face. The expression speaks so loudly of love as to be almost audible. In my role at the White House, my goal had been to have for all women the same kind of caring concern Mother Teresa possesses, even when I might be poles apart from them politically and philosophically, and even when they were publicly critical of me.

On the floor was an oval braided rug, and on the couch were patchwork pillows made especially for my office by an elderly woman from Pennsylvania. These were some of the "homey" touches for which I was ridiculed in a nationally syndicated newspaper article. Of course, the prose of that story was very sophisticated, yet it was easy to recognize the sarcasm between the lines. Speaking of me, the article said, "Her rhetoric, however, is as traditional as her hairstyle." The reporter obviously had wished to present me to readers as old-fashioned, and I suppose it stung a little. But at least she was simply reflecting her own bias and not misquoting me, as sometimes had happened.

Memories of my critics over the past year have been more than offset by all the wonderful supportive letters. Nearly a thousand flooded my mail after I was interviewed on Dr. James Dobson's "Focus on the Family" radio program. I treasure those letters from all types of women—homemakers and career women. A few came from men as well, and I value them also.

When I was appointed by President Ronald Reagan in September of 1982 to serve in the office of Public Liaison at the White

House, I was specifically assigned responsibility for outreach to women's organizations representing interests and viewpoints as varied and diverse as women themselves. I would serve under Elizabeth Dole, who directed the entire Public Liaison Department in the White House at that time.

Of course, it would have been an impossible task for one person to have frequent personal contact with *all* the hundreds of those organizations across the nation. Our office had, however, been able to communicate with a vast number of them, and, with the exception of a couple of the very vocal, critical groups, we had enjoyed a good working relationship. Several representatives of the more strident national feminists' organizations, presenting themselves as *the* voice of women, saw my well-known Christian views, my choice of having been a work-at-home mother for many years, and my not having been active in the "women's movement" as disqualifying me for the position. Mainstream women and I communicated very well. Even some of the women who disagreed were willing to join forces on areas of common concern with the Administration, and I appreciated their cooperation.

When commissioned to work with women in these volatile times, I knew I'd be on a political "hot seat," but I hadn't expected to acquire such a deep feeling for some of the personal inner needs of women. As I worked in the areas of legal and economic concerns, I discovered within me a growing awareness of an even more important need of women—something far beyond equal rights.

Few women can honestly say that at some time in their lives they have not been treated in an unjust or inequitable manner. In one way or another, most have had to face the old double standard or have been treated with a lack of respect as persons with value and worth equal to that of men. Certainly, justifiable reasons do exist for dissatisfaction and desire for change in our society.

As a result of the cries for change, much has already been accomplished. Old laws have been changed and new laws have been passed. In some instances, old attitudes have been exchanged for new ones. Some barriers have been removed, and some doors of opportunity opened.

However, the voices of unrest and dissatisfaction continue

to surround us. The drumbeat of protest goes on—sometimes for good and valid reasons and sometimes out of sheer emotion, rebellion, and many times, unfortunately, out of not knowing how else to resolve the confusion of new self-awareness.

Embarking on a journey in search of identity, women have often been diverted to the wrong course by beckoning lighthouses along the way—the lighthouse of developing talents and abilities, the lighthouse of equal treatment and career opportunities, and the lighthouse of liberation. Sometimes these beacons have even enticed them to give up home, marriage, and family in order to search for identity and fulfillment.

Some of these lighthouses represent just and noble causes. Some do not. But none of these guiding lights charts the course to true identity and fulfillment as women, as human beings— very special human beings. *There is more to be found than they can offer.*

It is in hope of charting a course to that "something more" that I write this book. The trials and tribulations, the joys and sorrows, the seasons of my life—as a farm girl left motherless at thirteen; as a struggling single parent; as homemaker and mother to six children; as co-founder of a small business; as supportive wife of a politician for twenty-five years; as assistant to my husband in his Senate office; and as professional staffer at the White House—all these experiences have had a part in shaping and molding me into the woman, the person, I am today.

And along the way I have found the most important ingredient of all, the one that tells me who I am and makes me whole. I want to share that discovery with all persons who are searching and especially those who are privileged to have been created "woman."

Those who read this book looking for partisan politics will be disappointed. Those seeking what they would call hard-core, heartless conservative rhetoric will find none. Those watching for the rigid call to unthinking submission will be surprised.

I hope that what those who search the pages of this book *do* find is personhood and peace.

The Subject Was Women . . .

Despite my thirty years of research into the
feminine soul, I have not yet been able to
answer the great question that has never
been answered: What does a woman want?

Sigmund Freud

In the hallway outside the Cabinet Room and the Oval Office, most times one could sense a lingering quietness, almost a reverential awe. As I opened the door of the Cabinet Room that afternoon, I saw that it was already nearly filled with people, most of whom I knew or at least recognized. I had been to this room many times, yet it still aroused a special feeling within me.

Rich brown leather chairs ringed the long, polished elliptical wooden table. Brass name plates on the top back of each chair designated the cabinet secretaries and close members of President Reagan's senior staff who customarily occupied those seats. On the far side of the table, with its back to the full-length sunlit windows, one chair—taller and more dominant—was set apart. That was the chair for the president of the United States. Across from it was a seat for the vice president.

Often since I had come to work at the White House, I had taken friends and associates on personal tours of the West Wing, as we were permitted to do after seven o'clock most evenings. Usually I was bone-weary by then, having started my daily routine at six in the morning or earlier. However, my fatigue nearly always gave way to pleasure in the obvious enjoyment and appreciation on people's faces at seeing the Oval Office, the Cabinet Room, and the Roosevelt Room. So many momentous discussions had been held here and decisions made that determined not only national, but world, history. On television news, the White House and the people in it appear larger than life. But, of course, that is a false perception. These are just real places filled with real people who are just ordinary human beings in extraordinary positions, their lives intertwining with history in the making. One's surroundings can come to seem somewhat commonplace through day-after-day familiarity, but the White House was a place unique unto itself. I wondered if everyone working here viewed it that way. I hoped so.

As I moved into the room, I nodded and spoke to those I knew well. All seemed to be engaged in their own private conversations. The summons to join other support staff for this gathering had come only hours earlier, and all I knew about this Cabinet meeting was that the subject was women.

According to the political pundits and media dispensers of conventional wisdom, this was *the* current political issue—"women." Women were, supposedly, the people with whom Ronald Reagan was in trouble. And according to one columnist, this president "would suffer defeat in 1984 at the hands of America's disgruntled women." I had come to feel this analysis and others like it were simplistic and exaggerated, doing more to create public opinion and confusion than to report it.

I prepared to be seated in one of the chairs against the wall for staff members. As he reached his chair directly in front of me, Vice President Bush turned and said, "Hi, Dee. How are things in Iowa?" We talked briefly about politics in my home state. It held special interest for him since he and his wife, Barbara, had come to know very well the cities, small towns, and people of Iowa through his intense campaign there for the Presidency in 1980. Many observers believed that the strong support and the victory Bush had garnered in the early Iowa Republican caucuses had given him his biggest boost, leading to his selection as running mate by Ronald Reagan at the August 1980 Republican National Convention in Detroit.

The room quieted. Everyone moved into position as President Reagan entered through the door on the right wall. That door led from his secretary's office, sandwiched between this room and the Oval Office. He took his seat, nodded, and said hello to everyone around the table, signifying his readiness to begin. His momentary glance of acknowledgment and wink of personal greeting from across the room gave me a warm feeling. Without apology, I confess I have a great admiration for this president— and a respect that grew during the months I had observed him firsthand here at the White House.

The president then deferred to Attorney General William French Smith, on his right, who was to chair the meeting that day. The purpose of this session, Smith stated, was to discuss the recent report on the administration's efforts to identify the yet remaining sections of the federal code that contained sex-biased language.

In recent weeks a former employee of the Justice Department, Barbara Honegger, had been much in the news—in fact, *very* much in the news. The "Barbara Honegger incident" had become the big political story of the month in this city of the instant celebrity, where news items and people could monopolize media interest and attention overnight and be forgotten just as quickly.

Arriving in Washington, D.C., in the winter of 1978, after my husband, Roger, had been elected to the United States Senate from Iowa, I had been amazed at the tremendous impact of the Washington-based media upon news reports carried across the country. Of course, local news in Washington is national news, since this is the seat of government power. However, if something is reported incompletely, or inaccurately, by just one reporter or commentator here in Washington, it is almost certain to be repeated, reported, and believed by millions of Americans. The power of the press in this city is tremendous. If elected officials allow the ever-present danger of "bad press" to dominate their concerns, there can be devastating effects upon the manner in which they execute the duties of their office.

In the case of Ms. Honegger, it seems she had worked on a special project at the Justice Department in which an extensive search was being conducted to identify still-existent vestiges of discrimination in the federal code and regulations. President Reagan created the Task Force on Legal Equity by executive order on December 21, 1981, to activate this project.

After resigning shortly prior to the expiration of her political appointment at the department, Ms. Honegger had now publicly accused President Reagan and his administration of not being sincerely concerned about the interests of women. She charged that the work of the task force had been put on the back burner, more or less, and that there had been no action on the group's recent report delivered to the White House.[1] The media had loved the implications of the story, and those feminist leaders with anti-Reagan sentiments had jumped on it, welcoming her with open arms.

As our meeting began, Attorney General Smith said that our agenda called for the Justice Department report in question to be reviewed by Assistant Attorney General Brad Reynolds. While Smith gave some of the background information, my mind raced over the events of the last few weeks.

Viewing Ms. Honegger on some of the TV talk shows and interviews, I vaguely remembered seeing her and saying hello one time at some public event. Later I had seen her name on documents that had come across my desk, papers having to do with this Justice Department initiative. I had read the extensive article in the *Washington Post* under Ms. Honegger's name on the guest editorial page and the many follow-up news stories. And, to be perfectly honest about it, though I believed the premise for her attacks to be totally inaccurate, I had felt some compassion for her. Having also read some of her own personal writings and the newspaper stories about her interests, I knew of her involvement and study in the areas of the occult: astral projection, something she termed "coincidences," and what sounded like a mix of astrology and numerology.

It was obvious that this woman was searching for something—truth, meaning to life, perhaps? I did not know, but I did not believe that her personal intent was to do harm to the president. And I sensed that her momentary "place in the sun" would quickly wane.

As I refocused my attention upon the activities in the Cabinet Room, Attorney General Smith was recounting some of the other actions under the present administration that especially benefited women. I knew the list well. I had recited it countless times during the last months in speaking to women's groups and in media interviews across the country. Through intensive study after assuming my White House staff position, I had been amazed at just how much had already been done affecting women positively, but which virtually no one was talking about. All that could be heard was the loud cacophony of criticism. I wondered why.

The charges of the detractors were very familiar to me. As I mentioned in my preface, I had become the focal point of the political critics' barbs and the militant feminists' attacks after my appointment as Special Assistant to the President for Public Liaison early in September of 1982. It was a position I had not sought and had not accepted without deliberation, and I had known it would be a political "hot seat," since my area of liaison responsibility would be to women's organizations. But the intensity of the attack was even greater and more vicious than I had anticipated.

I found it curious. It seemed that many of the anti-Reagan feminists thought the fact that I had not been supportive of the Equal Rights Amendment and was pro-life should have ruled me out for the position—as though holding those views made one anti-women. It was especially ironic to me since those were the very same positions held by the president, positions well known to the American voters when they had elected him less than two years before. It seemed only common sense that he would be inclined to appoint someone who supported his views on most issues.

The objecting feminists spoke as though only a woman who qualified as a feminist by their definition and who was active in the "women's movement" could be a capable liaison person to women's organizations. Of course, even being identified as a feminist involves semantics, since so many definitions of the word *feminist* exist. In earlier years the term described a person who supported women's suffrage and who demanded that women be given the right to vote, a cause with which I and most everyone today would be in accord. To some the term simply meant one who had the desire to see women treated fairly and justly, not discriminated against or treated poorly just because of gender alone. There again, my active support would have to be added. But in the more radical position today, being a feminist means that one favors treating women as being identical to men, among other things, supporting their inclusion in the military draft and sending them into combat. Additionally, this definition means supporting abortion and lesbian rights.

However, women's organizations are as diverse in their views, goals, and interests as are American women. And no *one* group is representative of all women. We are not a monolith.

I knew that the more conservative women's organizations had not been pleased, nor had I, with the views espoused by some of the women President Carter had appointed to his administration. However, appointment choices are the prerogative of a president, and I respected that. That was how politics and government worked. And in the twenty-plus years that I had been involved in organizational and campaign politics, I had learned that instead of acting outraged and shocked, the positive thing to do was to go to work within the system and get the people with whom you agreed elected.

The formal review of the code search having been completed, the term *gender gap* caught my ear as someone around the Cabinet Room table started informally discussing the "women issue." It seems that about 125 items had been noted by the report, although some of them already had been corrected and others were included in a bill that had been introduced in Congress with the administration's support. It was then generally agreed—as everyone familiar with the subject already knew—that there was nothing of great import included in the list, except those sections of the code dealing with drafting women and placing those serving in the military into combat.

When the section regarding the military was discussed, the president said, as he had publicly stated before, "I suppose it will bring down the wrath of women all over the place on me, but I just can't support sending women into combat." I thought, as a woman, I agree with him and appreciate his stand, as I felt most Americans would, especially those with daughters.

Looking at the participants around the room, I sensed a great frustration among them. The question, spoken or unspoken, was, "What can we do about the women?" Though there was an acknowledged political consideration, there was also sincerity.

Most of the people in the room were men, but certainly not all. Secretary of Transportation Elizabeth Dole and Secretary of Health and Human Services Margaret Heckler were the most notable exceptions. Both were very professionally skilled and competent women. Both were very sensitive to the needs of today's women and had championed their causes in the past. They knew well this president's record regarding women. And, although they didn't agree with him on everything, they were still very supportive. That should say something.

Yet why all this confusion? Why were the critics so shrill? Why did almost everyone in the administration run in circles when the term *gender gap* was reported or printed, or thrown out like a projectile by political opponents, in describing President Reagan's lesser support from women?

However, where the subject of women was concerned, frustration wasn't just the administration's private property. The more militant feminists also were obviously frustrated. The moderate and conservative women were frustrated at times, as were the men of the country who no longer knew how they should, or even wanted to, relate to women. Political candidates were confused about what to say that would be adequate for women. And some of our nation's children were experiencing problems in their homes, resulting from the stresses and strains between their mothers and fathers arising from this new self-awareness of women.

What was the main problem? Why all the alienation, hostility, and division between women with different points of view? What was the real need of women today?

As the meeting ran over the allotted hour, the president reached into the jellybean jar in front of him, took a handful, and started it around the table, with almost everyone partaking. Glancing past him through the windows on the far side of the room, I could see the calm, well-manicured serenity of the Rose Garden. What great contrast to the frustration within the room itself!

The decision was made, with no real disharmony, that, except for those in the draft and combat sections, most of the statute language changes would be supported. One person said that if women wanted to be treated identically to men, then there shouldn't be any distinctions favoring women. There should be no more Women's Bureau at the Department of Labor, unless of course, a Men's Bureau was established. Someone else quickly interjected that this would be a foolish consistency, to say the least. And on it went.

Watching and listening to the discussion confirmed to me all over again something I had long experienced: most men really do not understand women. Were a few of the men in this administration, in today's vernacular, "chauvinistic"? I am sure they were, as some men in previous administrations had been. Most of them were not, however. I was witnessing some genuine concern. And it was interesting to note that often—though certainly not always—those persons publicly credited with being true women's advocates, in reality were not. And those under the most attack for being against women's rights were the most fair and equitable in their attitudes and actions toward women. Strange.

During the course of this meeting, I had watched the president and studied his face. He listened intently, as is his custom, as all the information was presented to him, but I noticed that he had been quieter than usual. I thought how frustrated he must have been over this entire women's flap in the press.

Having been around him, I knew him to be fair and equitable to all, men and women—courtly in his gentlemanly way, yes; but patronizing, never. How discouraging it must have been to be accused of lacking concern and then ridiculed when he attempted to communicate his concern.

As governor of California, he had taken the lead on numerous things to bring fairness to women in many areas, and still he was being portrayed as the enemy by some women. That desire to bring equity was not unique to President Reagan. Though not always by the same means, but certainly by intent, Presidents Ford and Carter had actively sought the same thing. Indeed, a statute and regulation search was in progress during their administrations also.

The president's aides fidgeted as the meeting was running twenty minutes overtime, a real problem in a realm where literally each minute is scheduled and everyone is a captive of the clock.

As the president prepared to leave, his parting words revealed the reason for the faraway look I had noticed in his eyes once or twice during the meeting. "I just talked to Secretary Shultz on the telephone," he said, "and he just 'terminated' a meeting with Gromyko." The president went on to say that Secretary of State George Shultz had asked Soviet Foreign Minister Andrei Gromyko about the recent Soviet downing of the Korean jetliner. Gromyko had refused to say anything more than he had the day before when he had pronounced the matter closed. This meeting had taken place in Madrid where the Conference on Security and Cooperation in Europe was being held. In the news accounts later in the day, Shultz characterized as unacceptable and absurd Gromyko's explanation of the shooting down of the Korean airliner in which 269 persons died. This had undoubtedly been playing on the president's mind intermittently during this entire meeting.

This terse encounter between these representatives of the two great world powers could have an impact on international affairs and, therefore, affect the world community. Ironically, at the same time, here in this room had gathered most of the administrative leaders of one of those world powers, the United States, the leading nation of the free world, and they had spent all their time struggling with the "women's issue." Even stranger was the fact that one of the administration's severe critics, Judy Goldsmith, president of NOW (National Organization for Women), had already written off as "fluff" the Justice Department project which was the central focus of the meeting.[2] And adding to the incongruity was the fact that this was happening in a nation where women have more opportunities than anywhere else in the world.

What was the real problem? I was convinced that it did not lie in the often-heard complaints about failure of the ERA to pass and the lack of certain legislation. No, there was something more. It was elusive, nebulous, but there. What, in truth, was it?

Often Overlooked,
Mostly Undervalued

Social science affirms that a woman's place
in society marks the level of civilization.

Elizabeth Cady Stanton

The sound of women's voices lifted in song reached my ears that October morning as I was led through the maze of winding halls at the imposing Government Printing Office (GPO) complex in north-west Washington. I had been asked to address the GPO Women's Day assembly, filling in for my White House "boss," Elizabeth Dole, who had fallen victim to one of those tyrannical, unex-pected schedule demands over which we had no control. Because I was a last-minute replacement, my information about the group was sketchy.

As I prepared to go on stage and wait for my spot on the program, which was already in progress, I was briefed about the activity and the audience. This was an annual event and this year's assembly numbered about seven hundred women em-ployees, of whom the majority were black. Many were raising children alone, and President Reagan was not their favorite per-son. Well, that information was less than encouraging for a fea-tured speaker about to represent the Reagan administration.

Slipping across the platform as inconspicuously as possible, I took a chair. I searched my mind and heart for the right words and the best manner to approach this group. But I was unable to tune out the song or the singer who now had captured the rapt attention of the audience. The song was Helen Reddy's "I Am Woman." The singer was Imagene Stewart, a black woman minister from the D.C. area, with whom I have corresponded from time to time since that day.

Imagene sang with power and feeling. Her bounce and joy

were infectious. And one line of the lyrics really struck a responsive chord within me—"I am woman. I am invincible. I can do anything." I thought, "That's right. It's true. Women can—we can."

Looking out at that sea of faces, I saw women assembled for an event being held in their honor, for them to celebrate being women. Yet I sensed that many of them had to search hard to find something worth "celebrating" in their lives. My heart went out to them, for I had been there too, and I understood their heartaches and felt their hurts and frustrations.

The woman presenting me was very gracious in her introduction, and I found myself listening almost with embarrassment. Moving to the podium, I prayed for the ability to communicate some of my honest feelings. Formal speeches are hard for me, as is relating to people "in clumps." Sharing that, I said I thought of all of them as individuals. Behind each of their faces, I knew, there was a real human being, so I wanted to visit with them informally that morning.

I related the fact that I had just come from a breakfast gathering held in the basement of an inner city black church. A group called One Ministries serves breakfast to street people there three days a week after a time of fellowship, music, and worship. Most present that morning were men, black men, who had absolutely nothing in this world except themselves, for they lived on the streets of the city. I told the women that, as John Staggers, Jr., Director of One Ministries, had introduced me, I had felt very uncomfortable because of how I must have appeared to those desolate men. I said to the women who filled the GPO auditorium, "And I am sure I appear to you as someone who has always been on top of the heap—well-dressed, wife of a United States senator, serving at the White House. But let me tell you who I really am. I know firsthand that 'woman, she can do anything,' because there have been times when I have had to. No one has to convince me that women are capable of just about anything."

Confiding further, I said, "I was reared on a small Iowa farm, as a member of a family enduring rural post-depression poverty. As a child, I didn't realize that we were poor—at least by today's standards. I did know then that an orange was a big deal and that I had only two dresses. But, you know, we had each other and we had enough to live on, and everything was okay. Then my mother died when I was young, thirteen, and that brought tragedy into my life. I tried to help with my brother who was nine. I had some rough times.

"While Imagene was singing, 'I am woman, I am invincible, I can do anything,' I was sitting up here thinking that twenty-six years ago I wasn't a Special Assistant to the President. No, I was struggling to raise a child alone and was sometimes working at two or three jobs just to make ends meet. In addition, I'd made the mistake of an early, unfortunate marriage and gone through a divorce which I didn't believe was right, so my sense of failure was great and my self-esteem was very low.

"Later I met and married my husband, who had four young children. I raised them and have thought of them as my own for the last twenty-five years. A year and a half after we were married, we had a child, and five of the six children in our household were six years old or younger. I had my hands full—but my heart was full too, and I loved it."

Although there were many additional struggles and challenges of a different nature that I had faced later in life, I did not reach back into my past any further that morning. But I wanted to go far enough to let them know that I was no stranger to some of the hardships with which they were dealing. I went on to affirm them as women and encourage them to grow, to think big, and to believe that they could do it—because they could. I then spoke of current legislative and economic matters affecting women.

Typeline, the newspaper for U.S. Government Printing Office employees, printed my picture on the front page of the November 1982 issue, and the accompanying article included a number of quotes from that speech. The closing line read, "She [Jepsen] received a standing ovation from the capacity crowd."[1] That had been an unanticipated response. It wasn't that I had said anything great. I think they simply wanted someone to care, to understand, and to love them—which perhaps they sensed I did.

The response of the GPO women only confirmed something I had begun to sense very quickly after I assumed my duties in my new position working with women. Though I spent much of my time involved in and speaking on legal and economic issues affecting women, there seemed to be something else that many women were more eager to hear.

The month before the GPO Women's Day event, just weeks after coming to the White House, I had spoken at a regional meeting of the General Federated Women's Clubs in Maine. The close of my address focused on the value of women and the mistake of seeking our identity in any other person—husband or child—or in our vocation. Instead, I stressed that our identity lies in our value as human beings, individuals. That message of encouragement to develop our talents, to realize our importance to society, was a message of recognition of the worth of women that I would give today:

> Women are primarily responsible for passing on our culture, passing on our values and for shaping and molding the young lives of the leaders of tomorrow. We women have often been taken for granted, and seldom taken seriously by many in our society. What is needed now is healing, not more hostility. Hostility is not a solution, but a new problem. . . .
>
> Women who choose to be career homemakers, and that is what homemaking is—a career—need to know that they are making a major contribution, not only to their families, but to society. And these women should not feel guilt or societal pressure to prove their worth by joining the professional work force. And women who choose to pursue a career in the marketplace should not feel guilty or selfish. They need, also, to realize that they can take what are identified as "traditional values" in our society with them, wherever they play their role in life. Holding traditional values and pursuing a career outside the home are not mutually exclusive for women. Women can value marriage and family, hold moral values high, and still function in today's marketplace. In fact, those principles are sorely needed there.

I cautioned that as women moved into new areas of responsibility and activity in our changing society, they not diminish their womanhood: "We have, as women, been gifted with a greater sensitivity than most men, perhaps because we are the life-bearers. We have compassionate, caring natures. We don't see numbers and statistics. We see the lives behind them. Women bring a quality to life that men cannot duplicate. We have the capacity to love and to communicate that love. We are relational.

We bring out the best in people. It is a privilege to be a woman."

That message was to grow over the next year.

Later that evening, after I had retired, the telephone in my hotel room rang. On the other end of the line a woman's voice revealed deep emotion as she said, "I apologize for waking you, Mrs. Jepsen, but I just wanted to tell you that you touched my life tonight. Thank you." She went on to identify herself and we talked briefly. When I thanked her for her call and her comments, she said, "No, don't thank me. Just keep it up."

I never heard from that woman again and have no idea just what was stirring in the recesses of her heart or what words had spoken to her need. Lying in bed that night I mulled over that conversation. There is a deep hunger in women today which I was only beginning to realize.

When I said that women have often been taken for granted, and seldom taken seriously, I meant that some men held attitudes that lacked appreciation for the full value of women, and some women were guilty of the same offense. Many views and situations that society has accepted through the years really should not have been acceptable. The old double standard of conduct was dead wrong. It should have been unthinkable for wives to be treated like possessions by their husbands, rather than like human beings with equal worth. But it happened, and still does in some marriages today. The attitude—which, thank goodness, is changing—that a woman doing the same work as a man should be paid less was not only unfair, but illogical.

And unfortunately, the major impact women have on all of society has been either ignored or underrated. Taking ourselves too seriously can be destructive, but not seeing the significance of our contributions and, more important, our influence can be a fatal flaw. Poet and novelist Erica Jong says, "We women are brilliant at making the difficult look easy."[2] Have you ever watched, and listened, to a *man* trying to carry two overloaded sacks of groceries into the house, tell the kids to bring in their mittens from the car, call the dog back into his own yard, smile and return the neighbors' greeting, while struggling for the key, with the gallon of milk leaking, one child screaming because he dropped his ice cream cone, the other asking why puppies don't hatch out of eggs like chickies, and hearing the telephone ringing through the locked door, probably the plumber he has been trying to reach all day because none of the toilets will flush? What is commonplace for a woman can be a traumatic experience for a man, leaving him muttering for days.

My husband was in the insurance industry for twenty-some years and gave professional assistance to many men as they sought to plan their estates to the best advantage. I can recall that the general attitude years ago was that if a man left his estate to his work-at-home wife he was being generous. Many times he would not be so benevolent.

A sentiment generally accepted by professional planners was that "men loved their wives, but they 'looooved' their children." Therefore, it was considered sophisticated professional strategy to guide a client into placing his estate in a trust from which his wife would receive support funds, yet would not control. There are instances, primarily to save taxes, where this planning approach is not only advantageous but desirable for all concerned, including the wife. However, an additional reason was "hinted at": his children's financial security would not be dependent upon his wife, implying that "a woman doesn't possess the mature abilities to manage financial matters wisely."

Years ago this became a bone of contention between my husband and me whenever the topic came up in conversation. His total change of attitude on the subject in more recent times, in a very personal sense, speaks loudly of a heightened awareness of this old specious bias.

There had been no recognition given the fact that marriage is not just a mutual commitment, but an economic partnership, no matter what the division of labor may be. When a couple decides that the wife will stay in the home and work there as a career homemaker to care for the family, not only the couple but society needs to realize that she is making a major contribution.

For nearly twenty years, with the exception of co-founding a small business that I sold to a partner three years later, I chose to be a career homemaker. I can still recall the irritation I felt when I would cash a check and the salesperson would ask, "Do you work, or are you a housewife?" To which I would always emphatically reply, "Both."

At the White House, I repeatedly corrected my colleagues, both men and women, and my career women friends on an error which I knew was unintended: that of continually referring to homemakers as "non-working women." This was the innocent result of societal attitude-conditioning, and I had to keep reminding them to use the term "non-salaried women."

Coming from the Midwest where the work ethic is deeply ingrained in the fabric of both men and women, I was especially aware that referring to women who did not receive a regular salary as "non-working" certainly was a misnomer.

My growing-up years in Iowa, a farm state, provided me with a rich background and a solid base of reference that I have drawn upon over the years. They also gave me a deep appreciation of the key role played by rural women, not only in their homes, but in establishing and developing the family farms and small businesses of our country. These women have filled the gap. They have been whatever the need of the moment required, from business accountant to tractor driver, and everything in between. Of course, these duties were always in addition to their myriad tasks as homemakers, wives, and mothers.

In the July 1983 issue of *Glamour* magazine, Mary E. Stoltz, who lives in a small town in Wisconsin, wrote an article published on the "Viewpoint" page. Concerning the isolation of rural women, Stoltz wrote:

> I'm a member of a minority group that's neither recognized nor flourishing: the rural and semi-rural women of America. Our needs have gone untouched by the media, the government, and the Women's Movement itself. We haven't been ignored on purpose; however, in our isolation, we've never realized we could ask for help. And we need it. Oh, how we need it! . . . You pass through our lives on your way to and from somewhere. . . . If shown at all, rural women are portrayed on television or in films as outdated stereotypes: plump little elves in hair rollers, chenille robes and aprons. You don't hear about our problems in the news. As modern women, we're invisible.[3]

She goes on to say that her discomfort with rural life, which she used to blame on its shortcomings, she now realizes is caused by an identity problem.

All rural women may not share Stoltz's frustration. However, I am sure that many would appreciate being recognized, or at least acknowledged for their efforts. We often hear the farmers mentioned on the news, but seldom their vital partners.

This country's earlier rural women of pioneer days are the

subject of a current fascinating book, *Pioneer Women* by Joanna L. Stratton. President Reagan, in his radio address the Saturday before Mother's Day, 1983, quoting from the collection of memoirs in Stratton's book, spoke of the many contributions made by women, which are given but slight notice.

Later I had the privilege of lunching with the author and then introducing her to the president. Joanna, a delightful and intelligent young woman, compiled the book from a legacy of writings by women settlers in Kansas collected by her great-grandmother. She had found the writings in the attic of her grandmother's Victorian home in Topeka.

Most of us have never given much thought to the kinds of grim realities and formidable challenges these women faced:

> To the pioneer women, the day-to-day uncertainties of wilderness life proved especially harrowing. During the working hours of the day, her husband was frequently too far out of range to respond to any call for assistance. Furthermore, circumstances often required him to leave his family for days or weeks at a time. Setting off on trading or hunting expeditions, the frontiersman left his family unguarded with only the hope of his safe return.
>
> Such long absences were wearing for the waiting mother. Burdened with both the maintenance and the protection of the family homestead, she could rely on no one but herself. In these lonely circumstances, she fought the wilderness with her own imagination, skill, and common sense and determination.[4]

Arthur Schlesinger, Jr., wrote in his introduction to Stratton's book: "As my father dryly observed sixty years ago in *New Viewpoints in American History,* 'All of our great historians have been men and were likely therefore to be influenced by a *sex* interpretation of history all the more potent because unconscious.' "[5]

We owe those courageous women a debt of gratitude for helping to lay the foundation upon which later generations have continued to build.

The prairie was not the only frontier on which women of earlier days contended in this country. Today it is difficult for us to realize that women acquired the vote nationally only in 1920, with the ratification of the Nineteenth Amendment to the Constitution, although a number of states had granted them the franchise earlier.

As early as 1647, however, a "place and voyce" were demanded in the Maryland Assembly by Margaret Brent. And in 1776, Abigail Adams, wife of John Adams, second president of the United States, wrote to her husband in Philadelphia, where he was a delegate to the Continental Congress. She admonished him not to forget the ladies, stating, "If particular care and attention is not paid to the Laidies, we are determined to foment a Rebelion, and will not hold ourselves bound by any Laws in which we have no voice, or Representation."[6]

On the face of things, since women were not guaranteed the vote, it might appear that the framers of our Constitution did "forget the ladies." It must be remembered, however, that the "common good" was an underlying objective of that day, as the delegates undertook the Herculean task of constructing the framework of a new self-governing free nation. When the Constitution of the United States was ultimately brought forth, no one could quarrel with the fact that the "common good" of all, both men and women, was served.

As women continued to crusade for the vote in the 1800s, they were called suffragettes. They felt the vote was essential because basic decisions shaping the patterns of society were made in the political arena. The women believed that once the vote was gained, it could then be used to eliminate other discrimination.

Elizabeth Cady Stanton, an early feminist, was considered a radical by many in her day because of her efforts to win suffrage for women, as well as control of their own property, and the right to obtain a divorce on the grounds of brutality and drunkenness. She noted in the mid-1800s, "Woman's place in society marks the level of that civilization."

The trials and challenges faced by America's women down through our history may have been more perilous and basic than those confronting modern-day women. Yet twentieth-century standards have required many women today to struggle through a "wilderness" of their own. Women in our society have borne the brunt of an unconscious, or at least generally unacknowledged, societal bias. Even though in the 1900s women stepped in and filled the needs of the times of both world wars, educational institutions and the professions were still slow to open to them. Their efforts in World War I (1914–1918) were credited with swinging support toward the passage of the amendment granting women the vote in 1920. The passage of the Nineteenth Amendment came only after long and tireless years of struggle by many dedicated women.

World War II saw women assuming new work roles. However, in 1945, at the end of the war, our society entered what some have labeled the "Ozzie and Harriet" period of the overly romanticized, rose-covered cottage with the white picket fence. Unfortunately, as everyone happily sought to return to "hearth and home," it was soon apparent that the social myth that had been created did not deal with reality but instead raised false expectations in women. A trouble-free, blissful, "happily everafter" image of marriage, home, and family simply couldn't measure up, and women felt cheated. In their emptiness, they were uncertain if they had failed or if someone had failed them.

Simultaneously, as dreams shattered and bubbles of idyllic bliss burst, other cultural changes were taking place. The advent of time- and labor-saving appliances, drip-dry apparel, disposable diapers and other modern-day conveniences such as fast foods, one-stop shopping, and the like, lightened the burden of household maintenance and left women with more discretionary time. Television and its accompanying influences began to draw attention to a "better life" and the advantages of a second paycheck. At the same time, our culture had retained its time-honored and practical convention that a girl, who would undoubtedly marry and spend her time raising a family, had little need for education or training outside the home. With limited instruction, many women were ill-prepared to extend their activities beyond the home. Some felt controlled by the traditions of men, used by their husbands, and trapped in their homes. As husbands went off to do what society deemed the "important work," wives saw their men pursuing what were presumably "glamourous" lives, while they attended to dirty diapers, cluttered closets, and more free and empty time. Being very vulnerable, they felt they were merely the support system equipping men, who really didn't appreciate them. And, unfortunately, many men did *not*, in fact, appreciate them, either for what they did, or, more important, for who they were.

In a society that defines people through their work, their credentials, and the trappings of power, many women found themselves without definition. Since self-respect is affected by what we see reflected in the eyes of others, the societal bias silently directed toward women was robbing them of their self-esteem.

Though some women safely made the transition into this current new era, in many a deep need, as yet undefined, was revealed. The American woman was coming of age, and she didn't know who she was. She looked into the mirror and found the reflection blurred.

The time was ripe for the genesis of the modern-day "women's movement."

3

Feminine, *Femme Fatale,* or Feminist?

A real need among women is for identity.
Women may feel that position, role, or style
establishes "self," but *real* identity comes
with a deep sense of personal worth. As
soon as a woman knows that she has
personal worth, she is neither demeaned nor
exalted by position, role, or style.

Sallie Clingman

Jeanie's long hair tumbled forward as she leaned over my desk, the sincerity in her brown eyes, moistened by emotion, speaking more loudly than her words. She had come into my office that afternoon to attempt to express her feelings. The young girl in her was revealed as she rested her elbows on the desk and fidgeted self-consciously, though she had the appearance of a sophisticated, preppy, emerging young woman of the '80s.

Jeanie was a favorite of mine, a college student whose work as an intern at the White House had brought us into frequent contact. Her sensitivity and kind spirit had attracted me, though I perceived there were a number of areas where we undoubtedly held different views.

She had followed me back to the office from a White House briefing where I had addressed a coed group of three hundred university students. It had been quite a session! The lively question-and-answer dialogue had extended the program to more than twice its originally scheduled twenty minutes. The students were a spirited group and our animated interchange was confrontational at times.

Earlier that day, at another meeting, a member of the other political party had informed them that I was the "enemy" of women's rights. Since many of the students in this particular group came from a liberal background, that had just fueled the fires of debate. Frankly, I had enjoyed it and I think they had, too. In the end, they seemed to realize that I was a committed advocate of women, though we did not always agree. A difficult situation had turned out well.

Jeanie said, "I apologize for their rudeness. They shouldn't have been so aggressive."

I said, "That's all right. I didn't mind. They are searching, which is part of growing up, and I am glad they were honest."

"Well," she said, "you know when you talked about how sensitive young women are . . . how we get offended when we are called 'girls' or 'ladies,' even when it's well intended? Well, you know, I'm not sure what I am, a girl or a woman— or what?"

Revealed in the teary eyes of that lovely young woman was the "blurred reflection" she saw in her mirror. Her struggle for identity was nothing new. But in today's perspective it was more intense, more complex, more confused than in the young of earlier generations.

The debate about women has oftentimes been couched in confusion. The misplaced anger that Jeanie and her contemporaries had about being called "girls" or "ladies" on the one hand appeared ridiculous, yet on the other hand, disclosed their search for identity. As women, as individuals, they wanted to be taken seriously. They wanted to be respected and appreciated not only for their abilities and talents, but for their worth as human beings.

A counselor friend of mine once told me, "The mental image many women hold of themselves enslaves them. Their poor self-image is holding them captive." Yes, I thought, many women are living within an "invisible box," conforming themselves to the dimensions of their own self-image, as limiting as that might be. How many times that image has been influenced by the words that are spoken to us and about us.

Words do reflect attitudes, and attitudes are often more important than facts in directing our actions. To Jeanie and her friends, being addressed as "girls" or "ladies" spoke volumes concerning the image they believed was held of them by the users of the term. Some who are concerned about the attitudes held toward women, having observed the great influence words have in inhibiting women and producing unjust attitudes, have pushed for changes.

The quest for identity among women today has led some to go racing down the highway of their lives, knocking aside or running over everything and everyone in their path, yet all the while uncertain as to the destination of the route upon which they have embarked. Contemporary psychologist Rollo May said, "It is an old and ironic habit of human beings to run faster when we have lost our way."[1]

Considerable zealotry has been exhibited in the effort to change our societal attitudes through, among other means, changes in our English language. For example, though the generic terms *man* and *mankind* have been accepted, and certainly understood, historically as describing the entire human community, this is no longer the case. Sensitivity to the words that offend some women has had a noticeable effect. In the guidelines that McGraw-Hill Publishers issued its writers a few years ago were instructions advising the use of *humanity,* not *mankind.* Additionally, they advised using *the women* rather than *the girls or ladies.*[2]

While this approach has pleased some, it has offended others. A professional woman approached me at a public event recently to complain about all the "language engineering." She said, "This chairperson and fireperson stuff has gotten ridiculous. They can call me 'chairperson' when they take the 'male' out of female and the 'man' out of woman." She made her point well. It's as though equality and identity could be found in words alone.

Even Dr. Margaret Mead, noted anthropologist, says she has "no sympathy as a scholar for the amount of utter nonsense" spoken by some members of the women's liberation movement. "What in thunder is gained in reversing *God is he* into *God is she* except irritating people?" she asked. "It gets us nowhere. All you get with a reversal is the opposite again."[3]

Betty Friedan wrote in *The Feminine Mystique* that the "core of the problem of women today is not sexual but a problem of identity. . . ."[4] Though I disagree with much she has written, I support her thesis that many women have an identity problem.

The basic feminist message of this present era took shape from several influential books written in the '60s. *The Feminine Mystique* was certainly in the forefront, igniting the early activities of the feminist movement. As the feminist doctrine emerged in this and other writings, several feminist organizations were established and public consciousness of women's frustrations was raised. Unfortunately, though Friedan's book and others of the time were presented as dedicated to the betterment of women, their message gave women little positive direction in their newly launched quest for identity. Rather, the message confused many and increased the problems of some.

Friedan defined the "feminine mystique" as the social concept that woman's sole worth was to be found in the fulfillment of her physiological destiny as wife and mother. Such a view, she contended, confined women to the hopeless prison of femininity. For a woman to dream of escape would be a mere exercise in futility.

Is it any wonder that this message brought confusion to the hearts and minds of those women who had been satisfied in their roles as wives and mothers and who had been finding a creative fulfillment working in their homes?

Continuing, Friedan's message only exacerbated this new discontent. Men, she pointed out, could improve their status through their jobs and careers. Obviously, however, housework could not give a woman status; its position, in her view, was lowest of almost any work in society. Thus, a woman's only claim to status was in her husband's work.

Though the value of homemaking had not received the proper recognition it was due, Friedan's pronouncements just wiped out the vestiges of self-esteem held by some women in the home. Their vague feeling of inequality grew and they began to see themselves as less than important. As public acceptance of this feminist doctrine developed, many wives began to see themselves as "victims," and being a "victim" automatically implies someone must be "victimizing" you. That person, obviously, had to be the woman's husband. Many relationships and homes suffered, or were broken, as a result of the resentment festering in these newly marshaled women.

Additionally, women who saw themselves as wives and mothers began to feel they weren't very worthwhile if they did not move out into the marketplace and prove that they could do the "important work," or at least tangibly prove their value by receiving a salary check. Some feminists held femininity or womanliness in such contempt that they viewed it as weakness. Many wives and mothers allowed themselves to be intimidated to the point of near apology, as they felt forced to say, "Oh, I'm just a housewife."

Not helping in all the confusion about identity among women is the current orientation toward youth and beauty. Bombarded as we are on all sides by advertising, articles, and books about make-up, diets, beauty aids, and glamour, most of us feel we really can't measure up. The perfect "10," which society appears to revere, is always beyond the grasp of the best of us. And as each of us strives to retain her youth, old age looms as the ever-approaching enemy. Dr. James Dobson, psychologist and author, states, "The American culture puts physical attractiveness right at the top of the list of the attributes necessary for self-esteem and self-worth. If you look at advertisements particularly, there is one main message that comes through at all ages, and that is: if you're not beautiful, you're worthless."[5] While I would be the last one to discourage any woman from working to look her very best, I would also warn that if that is her only means of establishing identity, sooner or later she will be in trouble.

The changing seasons in our lives bring different looks. It is to be remembered that the best look is not necessarily the extremely slender look of youth. According to eating disorder experts, the starvation disease known as anorexia nervosa, which usually occurs in teenagers and young adults, is becoming more widespread among older women. This seems to be another indication of women's continued pursuit of that slender silhouette of youth.

In this search for identity, some women, rather than looking to their husbands or children, seek identity in their sexuality. But their *femme fatale* attitude of using seductivity to manipulate unfortunately results in their being viewed and exploited as sex objects. This is a one-way street to "nowheresville," causing them to lose not only their identity, but their self-respect as well.

One of the biggest money-making industries in this country today is the pornography industry. An industry of international dimensions, it profits by demeaning, degrading, and exploiting women. It makes an estimated $6 billion a year in the United States, pandering to depraved desires while influencing societal attitudes negatively toward women. The message that is communicated, without need for words, is that women are sex objects to be used and abused, certainly not respected as men's equals. The legacy of this abominable industry is the carnage of bruised and broken bodies and lives of women and children.

According to the National Federation for Decency, from 1964 to 1974 alone, rapes in the United States increased 139 percent. The organization cites this as evidence of a relationship between rape and relaxed restrictions on pornography.[6] Father Morton A. Hill, president of Morality in Media, comments, "The subterranean world of pornography knows no love, no marriage, no trust, no blessed motherhood; only darkness and mud. It cruelly strips woman bare of every vestige of her dignity, leaving her lying discarded as a useless object."[7] Sadly, women are not the only victims. Approximately 600,000 children are being exploited for profit annually by pornographers.[8]

The antipornography issue is one which all women—feminists, traditionalists, and all those in between—should unite and fight to combat. The use of women as sex objects permeates our advertising and entertainment industries as well, and we should make our voices heard in that area also.

But things are not all bad. Many positive things have resulted from women's new consciousness. Many new options are available for women to direct their lives and develop their talents and abilities. Barriers have been removed and opportunities opened in many areas of education and employment. And there is, indeed, a long list of legislative initiatives that have been passed into law in the last twenty years, specifically securing rights for women.

Women in our secular society need, in all justice, the legal, economic, political, educational, and social climate that provides them full opportunity to make choices—life choices. And then we should respect each other's choices.

To one degree or another, government plays a role in providing climates of opportunity. But the area of social climate is a matter of attitude, of heart. It is true that if the government approaches the other areas with consideration to the interests of women, public awareness is heightened. We cannot legislate attitudes, however, and attitudes cannot be forced. Even when something is legislated, not all abide by the letter and the spirit of the law. Stealing is outlawed; yet people steal every day.

Progress can be made in that critical area in which the greatest additional changes are yet needed, the matter of attitudes—the attitudes held by both men *and women* toward women. American women need recognition. Amazing things could happen if we were recognized for our equal value, as human beings, and recognized for the contributions we make to the entire fabric of our society—in the home, the professions, the marketplace, the community, politics, education, and on and on. Women's self-esteem would not present a problem, whatever life choices we make. And as the men in our lives recognized our true value, they would begin to look at us differently. Attitudes *could* be affected.

Recognition takes many forms. It can come in the form of a husband returning home from work, seeing his wife through new eyes, showing his awareness that her work too is very important and offering to help, or expressing his appreciation in some way. Recognition can come in the form of a boss noticing his secretary's hard work, acknowledging that she is the nerve center of the operation and really isn't paid enough, and then giving her a salary increase. Recognition can take the form of an employer considering a woman for a position never held by a woman before, in response to having noted her ability to handle the new challenge. Recognition can be a woman's male colleagues appreciating her as a human being, not forming their opinions of her in any way based on her gender.

Matters of attitude are very fragile. Human nature has a way of resisting when it is pushed, berated, and when demands are made upon it with great hostility: a counterforce develops. As an extreme element has insidiously crept into the fabric of the women's movement, it has become more aggressive and strident. The growing hostility has built walls of division between men and women, and between some women and other women.

In her autobiography, the early feminist Harriett Martineau said:

> Nobody can be further than I from being satisfied with the condition of my own sex, under the law and custom of my own country; but I decline all fellowship and co-operation with women of genius or otherwise favourable position who injure the cause by their personal tendencies. When I see an eloquent writer insinuating to everybody who comes across her that she is the victim of her husband's carelessness and cruelty, while he never spoke in his own defense: when I see her violating all good taste by her obtrusiveness in society, and oppressing everybody about her with her Epicurean selfishness every day, ... I feel to the bottom of my heart that she is the worst enemy of the cause she professes

to plead. . . . The best friends of the cause are the happy wives
or the busy, cheerful, satisfied single women, who have no injuries
of their own to avenge. . . .[9]

The anger which has fermented within so many of the leaders
of the feminist movement has been not only harmful to their
cause but to them as individuals. There are many who believe
that the ERA would have passed had not some of the more
radical elements surfaced in the movement. In some of their
material they talk about anger, and propose that women direct
that anger at those obstacles in their way and not at themselves
as women. But, as the saying goes, "Hate, like acid, damages
the vessel in which it is stored." On several occasions I have
been in meetings of professionals who could be considered
feminists and have seen some among them with joyless, tight-
mouthed faces. Their obvious animosity caused me to wonder,
Why do you hate me? I don't agree with you on everything,
but I don't dislike *you*.

In the last twenty years women have entered the work force
in record numbers for a variety of reasons. Opportunities opened
and barriers were removed in many areas; education became
more accessible; household maintenance took less time; financial
necessity required it; there was a desire to supplement family
income and increase the standard of living; more women were
raising children alone due to broken homes; there was a shift
in the economic base away from manufacturing and heavy industry toward service and technology; and women were seeking
further independence. Part-time work and work with flexible
hours is fulfilling and desirable to some women. Women now
comprise 40 percent of the work force.[10] Many of these women
have young children, although a large percentage say that they
would prefer to stay home, at least while their children are young,
if they had an economic choice.

Some women who are pursuing careers, striking out to seek
their identity in their credentials and angry at what they view
as past "male exploitation," have imitated the characteristics of
men. The determined tough-faced women who pursue what has
been labeled a "macho-feminist" course appear to be buying
into the male culture they found so offensive in men and are
setting aside their womanhood. Ironically, as they struggle to
define themselves, they are mimicking the men they resent.

No wonder there have been so many confused reactions to the "women's issue" among political candidates, public officials, people at the White House, and everywhere else. As a headline asked in one magazine I saw recently, "What Do the Women Want?" Listening and poring over great masses of feminist material does not reveal an answer to that question.

In reading many of the publications and books on the subject of women and the feminist movement, I was struck by the great profusion of words, words, words—words that seem so often to contradict themselves. Some people seem to think that women's answers are in career positions, as expressed by the headline "Happiness Is a Good Job." Others appear to think that political power is the answer; as another headline put it, "New Goal Is Clout via Unity." Another view presents education as the answer to all women's ills. It seems that one myth has been exchanged for another. First the ideal of marriage, home, and family was to bring idyllic bliss. Now, careers, education, power and serving "self" will produce a full and happy life. Neither is true.

Friedan thought the key to the trap of the feminine mystique was education.[11] Elitism is clearly harbored by some in the feminist movement who appear to worship at the altar of education and truly believe it opens the door of life. I discovered this in a firsthand way when I was appointed to my position as a Special Assistant to the President in the Public Liaison office. Critics of my appointment called attention to my having chosen to be a work-at-home wife and mother for nearly twenty years before coming to Washington and to my lack of a college degree. Some of the terms they used to describe me were "a sham," "worthless," and a "cipher." The fact that I had served as an unsalaried professional assistant to my husband in his Senate office for nearly four years did not seem to count. Neither, apparently, did all the years of experience in volunteer and administrative campaign work, co-founding a small business, the wealth of experience gained in managing an active household of six children, and the many activities involved as wife of a long-time public official. In fact, it was said that my appointment was like "giving them one of Nancy Reagan's old dresses."

The fault that was found in my lack of more formal education and professional, salaried work history actually proved helpful to me. It deepened my understanding and appreciation of the problems faced by so many women in their middle years, who, by necessity or by choice, enter the job market. Although they may lack some professional or formal job training through their background of life experiences, many of them have developed skills, abilities, and qualities of character that could not have been honed by textbooks alone.

Women with backgrounds similar to those just described often find prospective employers unappreciative of their value and talents. Many women have worked full time, and sometimes overtime, serving their communities in a variety of ways on a volunteer basis and have no salaried work history to offer in an employment interview. Although the value of education and professional training should never be downgraded, a wise interviewer is sensitive to these variances from the norm and knows when to set aside the rigid, sophisticated contemporary measuring stick in evaluating the qualifications of such women.

Sophistication appears to be another of our contemporary idols. We seem to have sacrificed simplicity on sophistication's altar and have come away lacking. We fail to see that this shiny veneer often masks an emptiness and lack of true self-worth.

The unimportance of sophistication was brought home to me two years ago at a Capitol Hill luncheon for Mother Teresa that was being held in the Senate Caucus Room in the Russell Building. Long an admirer of hers and her selfless work with the suffering in Calcutta, India, I felt honored to sit at the head table and was looking forward to hearing her speak.

All present were waiting eagerly for her arrival. In came this tiny woman, even smaller than I had expected, wearing that familiar blue and white habit, over it a gray sweater that had seen many better days, which she wore again to the White House the next day. As that little woman walked into the room, her bare feet in worn sandals, I saw some of the most powerful leaders in this country stand to their feet with tears in their eyes, just to be in her presence. She was a walking bundle of love and her dark brown eyes shone from that wrinkled, weatherworn face. She was embarrassed by our applause and we were humbled in her presence. We were humbled because we knew that, at best, we were all so full of ourselves.

As I listened that afternoon, I thought, "Don't forget this, Dee. Here in this little woman, who doesn't want a thing, never asked for anything for herself, never demanded anything, or shook her fist in anger, here's *real* power." It was a paradox. She has reached down into the gutter and loved and given. She has loved those the world sees as unlovable—the desolate, the dying—because they are created in the image of the God she serves. Ironically, seeking nothing for herself, she has been raised to the pinnacle of world recognition, received the Nobel Peace Prize, and is a figure known to most people, at least in the Western world, and revered by many. She has nothing, yet in a strange way, she has everything. Is she so unlike what womanhood should be?

Memories
and Motherhood

The women's liberation ideology teaches
women to seek their own self-fulfillment
over every other goal. Those who choose
to establish that as their priority are free
to make that choice. But that goal is simply
incompatible with a happy marriage and
motherhood.

Phyllis Schlafly

*How well I can remember Christmases when our children were young! Awak-*ening in the dark of early morning to the knocks of young fists on our bedroom door, Roger and I would hear giggles and shrieks of excitement and anticipation as we would tumble from bed, don robes and join the children. Unwrapping gifts was traditionally reserved for Christmas mornings, and the rule was that we had to be awakened to go down to the tree with them before the joyful event could commence. It was amazing how early they could get up when it was not something required of them.

As we joined them at the top of the big staircase of our German Tudor home and descended to the living room, the smell of turkey which had been baking slowly all night wafted up to greet our noses. We would peek out the full-length leaded glass windows on the landing, usually to be greeted by the view of a typical snowy landscape of Iowa winter. Those good times conjure up warm remembrances. Funny how, in my mind's eye, I can almost be back there again. How much I loved those family times. No matter what later life experiences they are measured against, they will always be very special, fulfilling in the deepest sense.

With the departure of our youngest child for college the same year Roger and I came to Washington, a new season of my life began to unfold. It is building its treasury of rich memories as well.

I think of my first big event with the president, after I had assumed my position at the White House. Since it was a scheduled activity that I had proposed, I was the "project officer" with responsibility to prepare the briefing papers and talking points for the president. As he addressed the nearly five hundred women in the East Room, I was standing by him and saw him looking down and reading some of the words I had written. I was struck by the magnitude of the moment, knowing that, for me, this was a memory of a lifetime in the making.

Yes, that was a rewarding experience, as were many to follow. But, I can honestly say that it was no more fulfilling than those days when I was home, managing a household and raising a family—just fulfilling in a different way. There are many types of fulfillment, just as there are many seasons in life.

The appreciation of marriage and motherhood, of homemaking and family life, prompted many women to fly to their defense in recent years when they felt the family was under attack.

In an article in the *Washington Times* on August 15, 1983, the late Anne Crutcher wrote about what appeared to her to be the convoluted reasoning within the women's movement. In obvious reference to the outrage of some feminists at a statement President Reagan made about the positive effect women have upon men, Crutcher said:

> The hypocrisies of the women's movement being as devious as they are, it has become an extreme affront to women to suggest, as past ages have so firmly believed, that woman's role in history includes civilizing men. . . .
>
> The women of the 19th century tended to blame men's behavior—beating up their wives, failing to support their children and the rest—on drink. Feminists in an era where both sexes drink, prefer to attribute male brutality to patriarchy, which the more openly ideological find inextricably linked with capitalism. As if both the 19th century women, trying to get the men out of the saloons via prohibition and the late 20th century women trying to curb male domestic aggressions through rape crisis centers and shelters for battered women were not both engaged in civilizing efforts!
>
> Besides turning their backs on women's civilizing mission toward the men in their lives, today's feminists, as represented in *Ms.* magazine, have turned their backs with special vigor on the hearth and nursery. Not only is abortion exalted above all other women's rights, but the care of home and children is looked down upon as unworthy of a woman's higher energies.[1]

It is true that the two previously valued occupations for women, motherhood and homemaking, have been devalued in recent years. As the "women's liberation movement" developed into a force of national impact and the push for the Equal Rights Amendment grew, a strong counterforce sprang up from the ranks of America's women.

Without question, Phyllis Schlafly and her Eagle Forum organization were among the strongest and most effective forces to speak out early against modern-day "women's lib," as Mrs. Schlafly referred to it. In her book *The Power of the Christian Woman*, she summarized her concerns about the destructive new attitudes she felt were developing because of the movement.

> A popular modern movie, *Kramer vs. Kramer*, shows the consequences of the ideology of women's lib. It tells the unhappy story of a wife walking out on her husband because she wanted to "know who she is." She thought she was missing out on something because she was "only" a wife and mother. She wanted to find "self-esteem" as a "whole person." After consulting with a psychiatrist and landing a job paying more than her hardworking, faithful husband earned, she thought she had found what she was looking for.
>
> But it didn't bring happiness. At the end of the movie, she was unhappy, the husband was unhappy, the child was unhappy. The marriage was irretrievably broken, the custody battle was bitter, and the child had only one parent. None of the usual causes of marriage failure was present: alcohol, adultery, violence, or financial problems. The only cause was the siren call of women's liberation which led the wife down the primrose path seeking her self-fulfillment above every other value. The movie's success can probably be laid to the fact that it touched one of the tenderest nerves of our current society.
>
> The women's liberation movement disregards, denigrates, and denies the created beginnings of woman and the creative essence of womanhood.[2]

Schlafly believes that rather than building up the flagging self-esteem held by some women, the movement contributed to its deterioration. She states further in her book, "The women's liberationist . . . is imprisoned by her own negative view of herself and of her place in the world around her." She goes on to describe an advertisement by a major women's liberation organization. The ad ran in newspapers, magazines, and on television stations around the country. Schlafly explains, "The advertisement showed a darling curlyheaded girl with the caption: 'This healthy normal baby has a handicap. She was born female.' "[3]

Many developed growing concern about the anti-family, anti-marriage, pro-lesbian sentiments of the feminist leadership. As force and counterforce grew in numbers and intensity of emotion, a great chasm of division developed. Organizations formed on each side of the debate.

Beverly LaHaye, a pro-family activist, founded the group called Concerned Women for America, which developed a flourishing membership. Some of the reasons for concern by women holding traditional values based on Judeo-Christian principles are best explained by looking at representative quotes and stories reprinted from radical feminist material and distributed by LaHaye's organization.

> "Marriage has existed for the benefit of men and has been a legally sanctioned method of control over women. . . . The end of the institution of marriage is a necessary condition for the liberation of women. Therefore, it is important for us to encourage women to leave their husbands and not to live individually with men. . . . We must work to destroy it [marriage]" (The Document, Declaration of Feminism, November, 1971).

> "We really don't know how to raise children. . . . The fact that children are raised in families means there's no equality. . . . In order to raise children with equality, we must take them away from families and raise them . . ." (Dr. Mary Jo Bane, associate director of Wellesley College's Center for Research on Women, *Tulsa Sunday World*, August 21, 1977).

> "By the year 2000 we will, I hope, raise our children to believe in human potential, not God . . ." (Gloria Steinem, editor of *Ms.* Magazine, *Saturday Review of Education*, March 1973).

> "No deity will save us, we must save ourselves. Promises of immortal salvation or fear of eternal damnation are both illusory and harmful" (Humanist Manifesto II, signed by Betty Friedan, Founder of National Organization of Women).

> "All of history must be rewritten in terms of the oppression of women. We must go back to ancient female religions (like witchcraft) . . ." (The Document, Declaration of Feminism).

> "*Los Angeles Times*, April 10, 1978, Santa Cruz: Nearly 400 women

picked different notes and held them, catching their breaths at different times so the sound droned unabated for five minutes. The eerie monotones from this congregation of sorts reverberated against the angular outside walls of the Theater of Performing Arts and filtered through clumps of tall pines on the UC Santa Cruz campus. The hymnic call was to the Goddess. Later in the day, encouraged by the beat of bongo drums, spontaneous groups of circling women danced barebreasted in scenes suggestive of frolicking wood nymphs. . . .

"More than a successful university extension course, however, the event was indicative of a burgeoning spiritual dimension to the women's liberation movement in America. . . .

"Christine Downing, head of San Diego State University's religious studies department, estimates that many—if not most—spiritually sensitive women in the women's movement are willing to replace the biblical God with a frankly pagan and polytheistic approach. . . . A Santa Cruz woman, Ebony of the Mountain, 38, said, 'Some of the women think of themselves as witches, but not all.' "

It was evident why the more conservative women in the countermovement would find the views expressed in those quotes threatening to their beliefs. Of course, not all women who considered themselves feminists would agree, nor appreciate, these extreme views either.

The major legislative goal of the women's liberation movement has been the passage of the Equal Rights Amendment (ERA) to the United States Constitution. The women's movement presented ERA as the means to achieve equality for all women. However, the countermovement saw it as fraught with legal dangers and believed that, if passed, it would foster social revolution within our American culture. Since the amendment was worded to require a sex-neutral, gender-free treatment of both men and women, women in the countermovement had concerns. They cited the fact that a legally mandated approach to both genders would render men and women not equal, but identical, under the law. Though there are differences of legal opinion, many experts on constitutional law, on both sides of the debate, agree with the opponents of ERA that many dramatic changes could result, such as: all state laws requiring husbands to support and provide a home for their wives and families would be invali-

dated; women would be required to be included in the draft
and in military combat; abortion on demand would be a legal
right at any stage of pregnancy; and changes would result in
many additional areas. There was concern that no longer could
any distinctions be made due to gender, nor could there be any
laws favoring women even when appropriate.

ERA was passed by Congress and sent to the states on March
22, 1972, with a seven-year time limit for ratification by the
necessary thirty-eight states. When support of the required number of states could not be obtained by March 22, 1979, the end
of the allotted seven years, the pro-ERA forces lobbied Congress
for a time extension.

Congress granted an extension until June 30, 1982. The ERA
again failed to receive the support of the required number of
states. Different reasons were given for its defeat: in-depth study
had surfaced many areas of legal effect not at first recognized;
the extremists within the pro-ERA forces defeated their own
cause with the public by their conduct; Phyllis Schlafly and her
STOP-ERA organization and many other anti-ERA forces made
an all-out effort to defeat it; and there was concern that power
would be shifted from the legislative branch of government
which is closer to the influence of the people, to the judicial
branch, as courts would rule on various resulting legal issues.

The counterliberationists cited the statutes now on the books
which have received little attention but legally insure many
rights to women. They judged the ERA not only unwise, but
unnecessary.

As the voices from the feminist movement came at them from
one direction and the voices of the countermovement came at
them from another, many women listened in confusion. They
listened and they looked around them for "role models." Who
had found *the* way? Is there someone I can model myself after?
And even there they found confusion.

I had reflected on this as I attended a luncheon honoring several
highly successful women shortly after I assumed the women's
liaison position. One of the honorees was Elizabeth Dole, who
is now Secretary of Transportation. At the time she was still
serving at the White House, and I was on her staff. We had
ridden over together so we could discuss business.

The event took place in one of the city's finest downtown

clubs and the company in attendance was prestigious. The room was filled with successful, high-powered Washington professional women.

As Elizabeth was introduced to make short remarks to the group, she was referred to as an outstanding "role model" for women, and that she certainly was. I not only admired her professional ability, but considered her a fine woman and a good friend. Yet, as I sat there the thought struck me: Most women would be very intimidated by the group of women assembled in this dining room. While Elizabeth is an outstanding "role model" for any woman choosing to pursue a full-time professional career, most women not only don't plan to be, but simply can't be Elizabeth Doles. In their abilities or in their choices of life pursuits, they will not be using those standards of success. Does it encourage the average woman today to have the Elizabeth Doles, the Margaret Hecklers, or the Justice Sandra O'Connors held up as examples of successful women, if there are no other women presented who have chosen different life roles? How do the full-time homemakers feel, or the women working part-time just to add to the family income?

It seemed to me women should have a balance of "role models." I was not sure the latter was being provided for today's women, since there is such media glorification of the "working woman" (signifying those who have full-time careers). Doesn't this lack of balance send a subliminal negative message to women? Studies show many women already have a low self-image. Realizing that they will never achieve success by the standards being presented, do they feel that they are less important—that they are insignificant to society?

A voice on behalf of women within the counterfeminist movement is that of pro-family activist Connaught Marshner. In a paper entitled "The Traditional Woman," she presented a view of some of the successes and accomplishments of women from a slightly different perspective than one usually encounters today. In her effort to defuse what she believes to be the adverse effects of the feminist movement upon the family, she asks:

> Who is the New Traditional Woman? She is a mother of the citizens of the 21st century. It is she who will more than anyone else transmit civilization and humanity to future generations, and

by her response to the challenges of life, determine whether America will be a strong, virtuous nation.

The New Traditional Woman is not the vicious cartoon that the feminist movement has made of wives and mothers. The New Traditional Woman is not the syrupy caricature that Hollywood of the 1950's beamed into our living rooms. She is new, because she is of the current era, with all its pressures and fast pace and rapid change. She is traditional because, in the face of unremitting cultural change, she is oriented around the eternal truths of faith and family. Her values are timeless and true to human nature.[4]

It seems that many women have a difficult time these days deciding what their personal choices should be. They also have a difficult time accepting and respecting the personal choices other women make. The somewhat elitist superior attitude some careerists cultivate either intimidates or incites anger in work-at-home, married women. Mothers who work outside the home and housewives sometimes view each other with harsh judgment.

In the August 1982 edition of the *Ladies' Home Journal,* a number of letters were published which had been received in response to an earlier article entitled "Women vs. Women: The New Cold War Between Housewives and Working Mothers." The magazine acknowledged that hundreds of "intelligent, lengthy and passionate" letters were received.

Nearly all who wrote declared that they felt "privileged" and "fulfilled" to be homemakers, but they protested vehemently against the demeaning by society of their role as nurturers of their children and capable managers of their homes. One reader wrote about leaving a very interesting full-time career position where she had commanded a high salary. Deciding to place her husband and family first, she said, had rewarded her with a relationship with her child and her husband that had never been so close.

This woman reflects the views held by a number of American women, even though there has been a great emphasis on full-time careers and the career woman. In the January 1984 issue of *Glamour* magazine, the results of an in-depth survey of American women were reported. In 1983, 62 percent of the women surveyed said they thought women should stay home if they have young children, although this figure had dropped from 69 percent who held those views in 1982.[5]

Another surprising fact is that, in spite of the feminist movement, more than 90 percent of the women wanted to marry and have children. Though some would have us believe that marriage and motherhood are "out of fashion," it seems that in reality, most of America's women don't agree, including many who would describe themselves as feminists.

There is something special about being a mother, as I can personally attest. And there is something special about mothers. When the television cameras focus on the burly tough hero of the football game, he is pictured holding up his fingers in the victory sign, smiling. What is it he says? "Hi, Mom." Moms *are* special.

Successful Failures

Money is a great and good thing. But it is
like an incomplete protein; unless other vital
ingredients are present also, it will not
benefit you very much.

Deborah Szekely

The Random House College Dictionary defines success as: suc-cess, n. 1. the favorable or prosperous termination of attempts or endeavors. 2. the attainment of wealth, position, honors, or the like. 3. a successful performance or achievement. 4. a thing or a person that is successful, etc.

Failure is defined as: *fail-ure,* n. 1. the act or an instance of failing or proving unsuccessful; lack of success. 2. non-performance of something due, required, or expected. 3. an insufficiency; a subnormal quantity or quality: the failure of the crops. 4. deterioration or decay, esp. of vigor, strength, etc.[1]

These two words are antonyms, words opposite in meaning to one another. "Successful failures" would appear to be a definite contradiction of terms, which would render the expression meaningless. Yet, I believe, in this paradoxical term lies truth, the most accurate description of the condition in which some of today's feminists find themselves.

Perhaps you have seen them. I know that I have—sitting in my office, at meetings, luncheons, seminars; their eyes hollow, sometimes cold and empty. They have all the trappings of success, but their faces betray their condition, the failure.

They had "bought into" what they understood the complete feminist program to be. They had gotten a good education, good grades. They had pursued a professional career. They had worked hard, very hard, and they are successful at that career. As the dictionary defines it, they had achieved success—that is, attained wealth (a reasonable financial condition), position, honors—and, of course, the status that goes with it all. In accord with the definition for success, they had achieved a favorable termination of their endeavors.

But their eyes asked questions—questions that are often unexpressed: Now what? Where is that great satisfying sense of fulfillment which was the assumed destination of this journey we embarked upon? The question in the title of singer Peggy Lee's song, which had been asked by some women working in the home—"Is That All There Is?"—applied to these successful careerists as well.

Betty Friedan's 1981 book, *The Second Stage*, a sequel to *The Feminine Mystique*, takes a look at the results of the feminist movement. While she recounts some of what she sees as the positive accomplishments, Friedan also acknowledges problems that have developed.

In the first chapter she relates that she had not intended to write another book. In her words,

> I am tired of the pragmatic, earthbound battles of the women's movement, tired of rhetoric. I want to live the rest of my life. [However,] . . . I have been nagged by a new, uneasy urgency that won't let me leave. Listening to my own daughter and sons, and others of their generation whom I meet, lecturing at universities or professional conferences or feminist networks around the country and around the world, I sense something *off*, out of focus, going wrong, in the terms by which they are trying to live the equality we fought for.
>
> From these daughters—getting older now, working so hard, determined not to be trapped as their mothers were, and expecting so much, taking for granted the opportunities we had to struggle for—I've begun to hear undertones of pain and puzzlement, a queasiness, an uneasiness, almost a bitterness that they hardly dare admit. As if with all those opportunities that we won for them, and envy them, how can they ask out loud certain questions, talk about certain other needs they aren't supposed to worry about—those old needs which shaped our lives, and trapped us, and against which we rebelled?[2]

Yes, there has been a growing disenchantment which Friedan and others recognize. The human inner needs had often been overlooked.

One woman who became involved in the feminist movement

in its early stages of development told me that she had come into it very angry, angry at the situations in her life, and at the men she felt had fostered them. However, she said, "I mellowed as I began to learn, to study, and to see some changes. But that wasn't true of everyone. Not everybody went through that maturing process. They stayed angry. Anger is really non-productive."

The emptiness and bitterness that is so recognizable in some older feminists has been a "turn-off" for some of the younger women today. The *New York Times Magazine* of October 17, 1982, reflected this in a series of interesting interviews with young women in their twenties. They acknowledged the fact that they were uncomfortable for various reasons with feminism: lesbianism, bitterness, radicalism, very liberal politics—elements they saw in some of those deeply into the movement. One twenty-three-year-old professional woman was quoted as saying, "My abandonment of feminism was a process of intellect. It was also a process of observation. Look around and you'll see some happy women, and then you'll see these bitter, bitter women. The unhappy women are all feminists. You'll find very few happy, enthusiastic, relaxed people who are ardent supporters of feminism. Feminists are really tortured people."[3] A number of these women do go on, however, to acknowledge their gratitude for the strides that have been made on behalf of women by their predecessors.

There are many reasons for the disenchantment that is surfacing. Some women had been looking for their identity in the wrong place before, only in their husbands and children. Now many merely shifted the search, seeking identity in their work—their careers. True identity is not to be found in either place.

Looking for our identity as John's wife or Mary's mother will bring disappointment—for John could die tomorrow and Mary could go away to school and make her own life. Then we are left alone without definition. If we seek our identity in our careers, we will find that also will bring disappointment. For one reason or another, the career may falter or become hollow. Again, we are without definition. It is a mistake to find our identity in our vocation, no matter what that vocation may be. The only place where true and lasting identity can be found is in our intrinsic value as a human being.

It is a very easy matter to take a deceptive detour if we start our journey without adequate direction. There are so many voices calling out conflicting directions to women today, and there have been some, obviously, erroneous turns taken by some in the feminist movement. Dr. Carson Daly, a brilliant young woman who teaches English at the University of Notre Dame, expressed her views about some of these wrong directions in an article, "The Feminist in the Family: The Femme Fatale?" Voicing concern that the modern militant feminist advocates total equality and interprets that to mean identicality of men and women, Daly said, "This is a mistake in logic, but is a disaster in practice," for these feminists, in seeking to make men and women similar, have presented the worst kind of sexism. As they would have women become more masculine, they have thereby implied that men are superior. She continues:

> Unfortunately, in their frenzied efforts to adopt male roles, feminists have demanded precisely the less healthful and less appealing aspects of men's lives for themselves . . . seek the ostensible privilege of arising at the crack of dawn, commuting two hours a day in rush-hour traffic, undergoing a grueling day at the office, arriving home late and harried . . . consider it a badge of honor to live the kind of executive existence that many males already agree is a dog's life—long on money, hours, prestige, ulcers, heart attacks, and alienation from the family, but short on leisure, self-cultivation, spiritual growth, close family ties, or a deep sense of self-worth.
> Even more disturbing is the choice of the militant feminists to imitate the very kind of masculine behavior which they condemned in the past and which, ironically, contributed to the rise of feminism. The feminists, who once denounced certain male injustices and strove to correct them are now advocating these very injustices for themselves. They denounce the societally-sanctioned double standard of sexual conduct, only to uphold no standard at all. . . . The feminists castigate the man who neglects his wife and family because of his job, but now are arguing for their own full-time careers even when they have small children. . . . In the most illogical, immoral, and unfathomable turnaround, the feminists argue that since society has traditionally been lenient on men who committed these sins, society should now encourage women to misbehave similarly. This is tantamount to the abolitionists' arguing that the very heinousness of whites owning black slaves necessitates blacks being allowed to own white ones. Such an argument

cuts the very legs of moral righteousness and intellectual respectability out from under militant feminism.[4]

Daly has made a good case. In a personal conversation, she said to me, "What they are doing is compounding evil. Men cursed and insulted us with their filthy language—so now we should do it? It is just as bad for us to do it, maybe worse. We're saying it was a terrible thing when the father cheated. Well, is it better if the mother cheats, too? It makes no sense. We have allowed our manners and our morals to be denigrated, to be lost in this search for betterment. It makes no sense. Our reasoning, it occurs to me, has been convoluted, totally distorted and twisted, as has our language. We have constructed a vocabulary of deception, as well."

One of the tragic aspects of the acceptance by women of the "new morality" (which is just the old immorality), or as Daly describes it, "no standards," is that they become the victims of their own fallacious freedom. When liberty becomes license, and the allure of sexual freedom draws women into a lifestyle of intimate relationships devoid of the commitment of marriage, the greatest degree of suffering is theirs, not the men's. They are left discarded and used, stripped of virtue, youth, and beauty. Their self-esteem is battered and bruised and they are emotionally injured, not to mention the possibility of their having to deal with unwanted pregnancy and disease. Is this freedom or foolishness? Whatever happened to reason and logic, to common sense?

Today's women are receiving all types of advice, as the following headlines attest: "The Total vs. Totaled Woman: She Still Has a Long Way to Go, Emotionally"; "The Sexual Revolution Has Gone Too Far: Liberation Is Fine, But I Now See That Junk Sex Is No Better Than Junk Food"; "Betty Furness Tells Women: Exude Confidence—Even If It Is Fake."[5] How do they decide where truth lies?

Here are some additional examples, and the views they present. "The Furious Feminist: Finding the Line Between Blame and Responsibility" states, ". . . some women who not so long ago felt angry about their second-class status in America have now concluded that any problems women have are primarily their own fault."[6] Another, headed "Frustration Deepens for Working

Women—Working Women Stymied" says, "And, though there are surely numerous exceptions, it does seem that women who want to excel at work must sacrifice family or social life. . . . Women's enhanced access to work has clearly lessened their economic dependence on men and abetted the doubling of the divorce rate since the mid-60s."[7] In an article captioned "Differing Views on Women's Road to Corporate Success," Alice Sargent, management consultant and author, is described as applauding women's efforts to make it. The article quotes Sargent as saying, in her book *The Androgynous Manager*, "I see high-level women with no time for friends and supporting gastro-intestinal doctors."[8]

The emotional, physical, and social effects of high-pressure, high-performance positions for women in the marketplace and stressful, emotion-laden attitudes held by some feminists have led some to cite the by-products of such lifestyles. Author Robert D. Foster states, "Leading health authorities have determined that the deeper cause of much illness is the emotional reactions to life. Prolonged bitter hatred can damage the brain, and can cause heart disorders, high blood pressure and acute indigestion—all severe enough to kill a person."[9] Doctors tell us that more women today suffer from stress-related illness than at any time in our history.

And the increase in suicides, as well as illnesses, has some experts concerned. These problems were addressed in a December 1983 *New York Times* article, "Divorce's Stress Exacts Long-Term Health Toll."

> Recent studies are expanding on earlier research showing that compared with the married, never-married and widowed, divorced adults have higher rates of emotional disturbance, accidental death and death from heart disease, cancer, pneumonia, high blood pressure and cirrhosis of the liver. . . . In comparison with the suicide rate for married women, which was the lowest, the rate was one and a half times higher for single women, more than twice as great for widowed women, and almost three and a half times higher for women who were separated or divorced.[10]

Again women hear conflicting voices. An article in *USA Today* appeared under the headline "Beef Up Your Ego, Women: Sugar,

Spice Doesn't Work." On the other hand, Alice Sargent, previously referred to in this chapter, expressed the hope that women "would be agents of change in the workplace, in part by keeping their values in sight."[11]

Yet another article, captioned "Women, Success and Cruelty," recounts its author's experience with a woman acquaintance who, she felt, had been cruel in her behavior toward a waiter at their luncheon. She concluded poignantly, "I had always hoped that, as women were let into the system, as we got our jobs and made our money, we would remember to be gentle with each other and certainly with those whose services our money would buy, always hoped that there was some way we could avoid imitating men's use of power. Can we not?"[12]

The unabated hunger and quest for power can do strange things to a person. Haven't feminists accused some men of falling victim to that trap of character weakness over the years? Ironic, is it not, if then the complainants fall prey to the snare of the same fowler?

The quest for personal power and the lack of conviction about the appropriate code of conduct they should pursue has led some women in the work force to be very hard, indeed, on other women. Many women have told me that they prefer to work with men rather than with other women. It is a strange anomaly that we are sometimes hardest on our own gender, rather than finding a kinship in cause.

There are many strange twists to the entire movement of women into the work force. One aspect not often thought of, since many of us did not live through the early 1900s, is recounted by Phyllis Schlafly in her December 1982 *Report:*

> Until the 20th century, women always participated in the labor force just like men, whether on the farm or in the craftsman's shop. It simply required the productive labor of both husband and wife, and their children too, to make ends meet. When the Industrial Revolution swept across America in the 19th century, women worked in the factories just like men.
>
> One of the greatest achievements of the American economic system is that, by the end of World War I, our productivity had increased so much that the average working man was able to bring home a wage sufficient that his wife did not have to labor in the factories, mines, or fields. "Female emancipation" meant free-

ing women from the harness of the labor force so that they could have a better quality of life in a home environment.

Over the last ten years, inflation and high taxes have cut so deeply into the take-home pay of the average working man that women are being pushed by the millions out of the home into the factories and even into the mines. Almost half of all American wives are now in the labor force.

The funny thing is that some people call this "liberation." They even brag about the higher and higher percentage of women in the labor force, as indicated by government statistics.[13]

Could it be that we have lost sight of the "quality of life" in our pursuit of the "quantity of life"?

As Schlafly acknowledges, many women today have no economic choice but to work outside the home. However, in balance, there is truth in the view of former Secretary of Commerce Juanita M. Kreps, who is reported to have said that one of the mistakes women have made is to romanticize life in the rose-covered cottage and then, discovering their error, to proceed to romanticize life in the working world.

Reality has a way of "coming home"—and of coming to the marketplace also.

One reality that many working women have come to recognize, as one of my career woman friends puts it, is that "they need a wife." They need what wives have been to husbands through the years: someone to create diversions—cultural, entertaining, educational, refreshing; someone to bring balance into their lives—pleasant interludes, a break from the stress of careers; someone to share and care and meet basic needs.

An important element of life has been lost as women have been caught up in their own careers and the demands of those careers—not only for their time, but their attention and their energy. The warm, soothing atmosphere that helps make a house a home and a refuge from the stress and strain of the world has all but disappeared. If they are married, what they often find at home instead is a weary husband who needs the same things they do. Some working wives have managed to balance these things out to their satisfaction, but it is a challenge nonetheless.

For women with children at home the challenge is even greater.

They are torn in three different directions. They want to be the best full-time career women. They want to be ideal wives. They want to be good mothers. But each day comes with only a certain supply of energy, and only a certain amount of time. And ever-present in these women's minds are the questions: How do I best divide it up? and, What if there is not enough to go around?

In this country we live in an era of very high expectations. Our culture of material abundance, our advertising, television— all contribute to raising our expectations to an unrealistic level. We set ourselves up for failure.

The latest buzz word to describe the woman who has and does it all—and does it well—is "superwoman." In stark reality there are no real "superwomen." We are all human. We are not flesh-and-blood machines. And if, for a time, we are able to live as though we are, what is the point anyway?

In a 1982 *New York Times Magazine* article, "Careers and the Lure of Motherhood," the author commented,

> People say to me: "You go to school, you have a great job, a wonderful child and a wonderful husband, and your house looks clean. Wow!" But what's interesting is that I'm not planning to do that anymore.
>
> I've done the Superwoman thing. And now that I know that I can do it, my question is: Do I want to do it? Do I want to live like that? Do I want to set the alarm for 2 A.M. and study until 4? And the answer is absolutely no![14]

The woman went on to say that the "quality" of the existence of herself and her family was now her concern and she was adjusting her life to better address that concern.

It is difficult to be a full-time career woman *and* a wife and mother. Juggling to keep three balls in the air, she may find one or more will come crashing down in the process.

I was fortunate when I started working full time in that we had no children at home and my husband and I were in the same type of work. Still, there were many challenges. And frankly, I thought at times how nice it would have been if someone had been at home to greet us with a nice meal when we both came in weary from twelve- or fourteen-hour days. How much more of a challenge it would have been to have children waiting there as well.

Knowing and working with Elizabeth Dole, as I mentioned earlier, led to my admiration for her and her ability. She and her husband, Senator Bob Dole, one of my husband's Senate colleagues, have a high-voltage two-career family without rival. I never cease to be amazed at their joint energy and drive. However, they have no children at home, which makes their lifestyle, though difficult, at least do-able.

The woman who replaced Elizabeth as the Director of the Office of Public Liaison at the White House, Faith Whittlesey, had a different set of circumstances with which to deal. Faith came to the White House after serving as the United States ambassador to Switzerland. She was a widow raising three children alone. Not only did I find that she was a very dedicated, loving mother, but an extremely competent professional. As an attorney, she had served in public office and had a long political career.

I felt for Faith as I watched her fill the role of mother and father to her family, as well as serve in one of the most intense professional pressure cookers in the world—the White House. It was not easy. And I empathized with her the times I knew she was bone weary and was going home to give time and attention to her children. It was frustrating at times I am sure, knowing that most of her male colleagues had someone to go home to, someone providing that haven for them that she was striving to provide for her young ones. It takes a special person to meet that kind of responsibility, and I considered it a privilege to have worked for two such fine, though uniquely different, women during my tenure at the White House.

Even though children present an additional challenge and responsibility in our lives, many childless women in their early thirties who have had full-time careers are having their own kind of "baby blues" and are now deciding to have children. And though women are more societally conditioned to work outside the home today, a *New York Times* poll in December 1983 shows 47 percent of all women would prefer to stay home and take care of house and family.[15] Women's nurturing instincts still do prevail.

The extreme feminist message that pointed to professional

careers as the ultimate in fulfillment found that the rhetoric was proving inconsistent with the reality of human nature.

Yes, as America's women have "come of age," they are faced with many yet unanswered questions and unsolved problems. We have spoken of the disenchantment with the feminist movement, the confusion in the hearts and minds of many women, the stresses and strains of their lives, the different voices which call to them from all sides, and the lack of clear direction.

We have talked about women who have accomplished what they thought they were supposed to do to succeed, but in the quality of whose "success" there dwelled a sense of "failure." For success, as defined by the world, is but one aspect of the whole of life. Many women with successful worldly careers find themselves "fragmented failures" at life. The pursuit of a worldly illusion of success often terminates in disappointment and feelings of betrayal.

Betty Friedan is right when she says, ". . . I sense something *off*, out of focus, going wrong. . . ."

6

Another Voice

I became totally convinced of one thing:
women needed something beyond equal
rights—something else, something deeper.

Dee Jepsen

"They don't speak for me." I had heard this statement so many times in the last year from women all across the country. Sometimes they expressed it in letters, sometimes in messages delivered face to face. That was the case this day. But the message was always basically the same. It came from all types of women, from women who played all kinds of life roles.

This time I heard the statement from an Iowa woman who came to shake my hand after I had completed my speech. She had a warm and friendly face, yet I heard irritation in her voice—a tone I sensed she used only after having given a matter due consideration. She was the chief executive officer of a substantial industrial firm in the community, the type of industry which would seem foreign to most women. And she filled her position well, having earned a great deal of admiration and respect from both men and women in her city.

She went on to explain, "I am certainly for equality and opportunity for women, for goodness sake, but the views voiced by some of these militant women today are just 'off the wall.' They surely don't speak for me, or for most American women; they are just making the loudest noise. The rest of us are too busy working and living our lives to talk back. But I just want you to know, they don't speak for most of us out here."

During the months at the White House, I had listened as this sentiment had come at me from all sides. Some of the same women who expressed disagreement with the radical feminists went on to say that neither were they completely comfortable with the conservative politics of many in the countermovement.

This was just another piece of the puzzle I had been trying to put together in my mind. What was the most basic need of women today? What was the root cause of both the emotional clamor of some and the undefined hunger in others? I became totally convinced of one thing: women needed something beyond equal rights—something else, something deeper. Equal rights is only a surface issue. Whether or not the ERA was ever passed was not the key issue. Even for those who believed passage of the ERA would be desirable, it could not bring the satisfaction and fulfillment they sought, or meet the basic need in their lives.

It had started with that telephone call to my hotel room in Maine about which I told you in an earlier chapter. It had come from the woman who wanted to tell me that something I said that evening in my speech had "touched her life," something I had said without realizing its impact. In the months that followed, I had considered and contemplated the great hunger I continually saw and heard expressed by women—a hunger for positive words, as they were reminded of their true value and importance as individuals. I came to several conclusions.

First, women had a deep need, unidentified in most, often concealed in the blue fog of deception which surrounds them today. Friedan called this mysterious malady a "problem that has no name."

Second, there was a need for another voice for women. The voices that were being heard were not enough.

And somehow, I sensed that in identifying the "problem that has no name" and in discovering its solution, there would arise another voice for women.

As I struggled through the morass of verbiage concerning women's issues that encompasses us today, I could see very clearly that the loudest voices belonged to some who were attempting to lead a revolution, but a revolution without true and honest direction. Their condition was reminiscent of the sentiment I recently saw expressed on a bumper sticker: "Don't follow me, I'm lost!"

True leadership inspires, motivates; it does not berate nor pressure. Leaders encourage; critics discourage. But it was the negative which I saw and heard, not the positive, and it put new tensions in women's lives. Although this is a free society, it is not a perfect one. Since equal opportunity doesn't mean equal results, could the demanding voices *ever* be appeased?

An improper mindset has evolved, negative, critical, destructive—a mindset that advocates evaluating all things with the question, "What's in it for me?" In practical life application, that simply does not work. Selfish people are lonely people. Selfishness satisfies only for the moment. Living just *for* yourself, you will eventually live just *by* yourself. Even when surrounded by people, you will be lonely. Talk of individual fulfillment is hollow and meaningless when you must step on others in your attempt to achieve it.

I have seen some career women who are truly professionals: capable, confident—and cordial in the process. I have also seen some who have made a profession out of being a woman: supersensitive to offense, with but a thin veneer covering the rage which, so obviously, lies just below the surface. Thinking themselves professional, they have encased their personality with their perception of professionalism's externals. In the process they have smothered their true potential—and, sadly, their womanhood. Their attitudes have destroyed their attributes.

Let us strip away the political, philosophical, and educational baggage that has accompanied so much of what has been said and done on behalf of women today. Some of those who are the loudest and most strident travel with so much baggage that they lose sight of the proclaimed object of their efforts—women.

Much has been done legally that needed to be done, without a doubt. In pursuit of fairness and justice, laws have been passed, laws have been changed, doors have been opened, barriers removed. Where there are remaining injustices, let's identify them and address them, speedily. But, please, let's not leave the American woman standing on the sidelines, forgotten. Let us not simply use her as a catalyst for political and social change that we may personally wish to foster. Let us not merely use her in our own pursuit of power or a following—a weapon stamped "clout," to be swung to and fro at our own political foes, then to be set aside, fragmented and confused, until we need to "use" her again.

"Woman" is special. Equal? Capable? Of course! But she is even more. Let us not lose sight of her true value—perhaps we never realized it was there.

Are women equal to men? Absolutely, and then some. But then, why haven't we noticed? Why hasn't someone called it to our attention? Why have attitudes in our society been distorted and the full value of women overlooked? I'm not sure. However, let's *do* something about this glaring oversight now. But let us walk in the light of truth and honesty as we do, or our quest will have no lasting value.

Labeling each other liberal, conservative, feminist, traditionalist, only divides; it does not unite. People don't fit into neat, tidy little labeled boxes. We are not merchandise. We are human beings, unique, special—each one of us. We all have value. We are not of value just for the votes we represent. We are not of value just because of the title before our names, or the degrees after it. We are not of value just because we earn a large salary, or carry a briefcase, or head a large organization. We are of value, just because we *are.*

Every human being—man, woman, and child—has a need to be valued, to be loved, and to love, to be intimate and open with someone, to share his or her heart's secrets, to be able to let someone know "who he is" or "who she is," to be himself or herself without fear of being rejected. Now, let's ask ourselves, does what today's women hear in the public forum offer them that kind of value? Let's think about what women are hearing today.

Today women hear: that the two traditionally prized and valued roles of mother and homemaker are really somewhat second-rate; that you really aren't worth much unless you complete and achieve great things in a career; that unless you can exchange your talents for dollars, perhaps you don't have any talents; that only a dullard would find true fulfillment in staying home with her children; that being of service to another means you are being "exploited" and are therefore a fool.

One of the things I proposed at the White House, which never got through the crush of "the urgent," was the idea that we should proclaim a Women's Recognition Day. This would be a day in which the country recognized the many contributions of all women: in the home, the professions, the work force, the communities, the churches, in education, in government— across the entire fabric of society. This day we would focus upon and recognize the contributions that receive little or no acclaim, and, in many cases, for which there is no payment.

Women's contributions are both vast and varied. Not only are women primarily responsible for passing on our culture and our values and shaping the lives of the leaders of tomorrow, but they also have profound influence. There is often more power in influence than there is in authority. Just because the "little woman" doesn't have the trappings of power or command a large salary, doesn't mean that she does not exercise profound influence. Now, I find the term *little woman* demeaning, although I know people who use it and intend no disrespect. But, the point is that the wife may be the pivot for the husband and the entire family.

The impact of this type of woman was expressed well on the television program *Firing Line*, in an exchange between attorney Harriet Pilpel and host William F. Buckley. An excerpt follows:

> MR. BUCKLEY: And I think the notion that women exercise only 10 percent of the critical decisions in the world I live in is preposterous. They exercise probably closer to 75 percent. . . . I mean that women make the crucial decisions. Now, they may not be the decision to go to war, but they are the decisions by which you and I are primarily governed. . . .
>
> MRS. PILPEL: Oh, it's like that story of the woman who said that she decided all the unimportant things and the man would decide all the important things, so she decided where they lived, where the kids went to school, how much money they would spend, where their vacation would be; and he decided what to do about the disarmament situation and the war on nuclear weapons?[1]

If this conversational interaction has elements with which you don't agree, fine. However, the point of women's influence in society is well made. Of course, I do not believe that women should be limited to this type of influence alone, or that they should be uninvolved and unheard in the public debate on the issues of the day. But, to ignore such profound influence on the innermost substance of our society would be myopic, indeed.

However important, the recognition of women's contributions and influence *alone* will not meet their deepest need. There is something more needed—"something" which is the source of true self-esteem; "something" which leads us to esteem others, even though we may not agree with them—and even when, by the world's standards, they are not worthy of esteem. The "something" is Someone, Jesus Christ—the true liberator.

It was only fourteen years ago that I met Him, at a point of deep need in my life. It was a time when everything I cared about seemed to be threatened, and the husband in whom I had sought my identity appeared to me more interested in politics and everything that goes with it than he was in me. That was traumatic, for my self-confidence and self-esteem had been tied to him and his opinion of me. Those were difficult days for both of us, but days for which I am now grateful. Because it was then that I looked beyond myself, beyond my husband, my children or any other persons, and met the Son of the living God.

It is not my intent in this book to share all the details about myself and my life. That is another story, for perhaps another time. It is my intent to share Him with you, to share with you the great love that He has for you, and the exciting adventure that it can be to walk with Him.

He has walked with me through the valleys of personal problems and the mountaintops of political and professional success. He has enabled me to love myself and to love others. He has enabled me to believe the impossible "possible" and has taken my fears from me. He has taught me how very special I am as a woman. He has made me whole.

Believing in Him, knowing Him, is not something that is set aside for just those who are cloistered away from the workaday, nitty-gritty of life. Not at all. This life with Him is not only the most fulfilling way to live, it is also the most practical. I find that many of the early feminists believed in Him also, having become involved in Charles Finney's revival in the early 1900s.

To those who would scoff, believing that God does not exist, is not able, or is not faithful, I would say, "You have an argument, but I have experienced His reality and His faithfulness. I could no more be convinced of your argument than someone 'in love' could be convinced that love does not exist. The beautiful thing is that this experience is available for any and all who are interested. But a clenched fist can't receive; if our hands are full of ourselves, God can't fill them.

The answer to women's needs today will not be found in dividing into two emotionally charged camps, glaring at each other, finding fault and placing blame. What we need is peace-makers, not power-seekers. The tension of division is destructive.

I believe that God wants to raise up today an army of women who will find their identity in Him. He does not seek to put down, but rather to build up. He can replace all the "how to" handbooks with the "Maker's manual"—the Bible, whose truths are timeless. I believe that He will raise up "another voice" for women, and that other voice will be that of all those special women who will heed His call to come and "follow Him."

Yes, there is a persistent problem women sense today, one that seems to have no name. Ah, but I have discovered its name. Its name is hunger, spiritual hunger. It is the cause of the gnaw-ing, yearning unrest in the heart of today's woman. And only He, our Lord Jesus Christ, can satisfy that spiritual hunger. Saint Augustine said it centuries ago: "Thou hast created us for thyself, and our heart cannot be quieted till it may find repose in thee."[2]

The Best-kept Secret

We search the world for truth,
We cull the good—the true—the beautiful,
From graven stone and written scroll,
And all the old flower-fields of soul;
And, weary seekers of the best,
We come back laden from our quest
To find that all the sages said
Is in the Book our mothers read.

John Greenleaf Whittier

It was about noon and the woman had decided to run out quickly and do the errand she had been putting off. She always tried to go and do her daily tasks in the community when there weren't many people around. Folks like to gossip, and there was always plenty to gossip about where she was concerned. Everyone in this small town knew about her, it seemed.

Those disdainful glances and whispers to each other behind raised hands hurt her to the core. But then, what could she do? Her life was a mess. She was the first to admit it. It seemed that she had broken all the rules, but eventually she was the one who had ended up broken. Oh, well, that was just the way it was. She had learned to live with it.

It was windy that day. And little spirals of dust whipped down the road in front of her. That, coupled with the glare of the midday sun, made it hard to see. As she drew closer to her destination, she noticed that someone was sitting on the stone wall encircling the well where she planned to fill her water pot before hurrying home. She had so hoped no one would be there. But at least she could see it was a man. The women hated her. And she had a way with men, anyway. It would be all right.

But as she drew nearer she could see that this was not a Samaritan from her village. This man was obviously a Jew; she could tell by his looks and his clothes. He appeared weary, as though he had stopped to rest at this place called Jacob's well.

As they nodded greetings, the man asked her if she would

give him a drink, a strange request coming from a Jew to a Samaritan. The Jews felt superior to the Samaritans and there was a deep religious and racial animosity between them. And besides, it was unheard-of for Jewish rabbis to speak to women in public, even their own wives and daughters, much less to a despised Samaritan woman. Why, the Jewish men even recited a prayer every day thanking God that they were not women. This was all strange, indeed.

So she told the man how surprised she was that he would ask her for water. And then he said something even stranger. "If you knew what a wonderful gift God has for you, and who I am, you would ask me for some *living* water!"

How odd! She observed that he didn't even have a bucket or a rope. Thinking she would put him in his place, she told him that he was implying that he was greater than their illustrious ancestors, after whom this well was named.

But that didn't stop him. He said, "But the water I give them becomes a perpetual spring within them, watering them forever with eternal life."

So she thought, Okay, I'll put him to the test. He *was* a strange one. She had known a lot of men, but this one was somehow different, an uncommon man. So she said, "Please, sir, give me some of that water! Then I'll never be thirsty again and won't have to make this long trip out here every day."

And he zeroed right in on her. He told her to go and get her husband. You see, that was her vulnerability, and she knew it.

She said, "But I'm not married."

Yet he came right back at her, "All too true! For you have had five husbands, and you aren't even married to the man you are living with now."

She knew he was different, but this was too much. How did he know this? Even the townsfolk had lost count of her husbands and her affairs. They just dismissed her as a woman of easy virtue. But this man—

She had by now noticed his eyes. What eyes! They seemed to look right through her, as if he could read her thoughts. Yet, there was a quality in his look that was tender, compassionate. This was all too much. He has to be a prophet, she thought; we Samaritans have had them in our ancestry.

So she told him she thought he must be a prophet—and then quickly tried to draw this religious man into a theological discussion about the proper place to worship. Was it on the mountain or in Jerusalem? But he would not be diverted into a philosophical discussion. He told her that the time was coming when there would no longer be concern about the proper place to worship. It was how we worshiped that counted, not where.

This small, dark-skinned woman looked up at him quizzically. Watching his eyes, she said, "Well, at least I know that the Messiah will come—the one they call the Christ—and when He does, He will explain everything to us."

Then this man, whose name was Jesus, said to her, "I am the Messiah."

Just at this moment His friends, the ones called the disciples, came back from their trip to get food and saw Him talking to the woman. They could neither believe it nor understand it. It was totally counter to the customs of their culture. But they said nothing to Him.

As they came up to Jesus, the woman left her water pot and ran into the village, calling out to anyone in earshot to come and listen to what she had to tell them. Here she was calling out to everyone, when only half an hour before she had been trying to slip by unnoticed. She said, "Come and meet a man who told me everything I ever did! Can this be the Messiah?"

The villagers came streaming out to meet Him and asked Him to stay, which He did, for two days. And many believed He was the Messiah because of the woman's report, "He told me everything I ever did."

After they had heard Him during the time of His stay, they said to her that they then believed, not just because of what she said, but because they had heard Him themselves. They said, "He is truly the Saviour of the world."[1]

Perhaps you wonder why I tell this nearly 2,000-year-old story now. What, after all, does it have to do with this modern-day world in which we live—with advanced science and education, hi-tech, and women's lib? Why is it significant? I tell it because echoing down through the centuries comes a very clear and profound statement. The best-kept secret of our day is that *Jesus valued women. He is the true liberator.*

For, you see, there are many things about the encounter with that poor, hurting woman which tell us so much—if we will only look and listen for truth. If we dare to look. If our own pride will allow us, momentarily, to set aside our own sophisticated opinions about the answers to life's questions. If we are willing to risk having our neat, "pat" answers and contemporary cultural constraints shattered. I can assure you, something so much better will be found.

Come with me, if you will, and walk through these next pages as we seek for truth together—the truth which you will so clearly hear saying: *it is a privilege to be woman.*

Women are special. They are loved and valued by the God of the universe. And the Son of that living God, Jesus, is our liberator, the one who can bring wholeness to our lives, wherever we may live them. He alone is the solution to "the problem that has no name" in women's lives. He alone can satisfy that "spiritual hunger," which is the problem identified.

First, let's look at that short encounter between the Samaritan woman and Jesus at the well that day. And let's see more closely what it says about Him, about women, and about us today.

For the first time Jesus directly revealed His true identity to someone, and that someone was a seeking woman. In the eyes of the Samaritans, her own people, she was a social outcast. And in the eyes of His people, the Jews, she was despicable. In His eyes she had value, she had worth, she had importance. *She had enough importance to Him that He told her who He was.* And she believed and ran and told others. What a tribute to her as a person, as a woman. That brief encounter changed her life. He told her that He knew her darkest secrets, yet He still chose to trust her with His fantastic secret. He gave her dignity.

You may say, that's fine if you believe all that, but what has that got to do with us today? Well, I can tell you, from experience, He still treats all of us with compassion and care today. I have found it true and so have hundreds of other women I know. Many of these women have achieved great "worldly" accomplishments, while others have achieved accomplishments unacknowledged by the world. They are not just the women the word *Christian* may conjure up in the minds of some of you, whatever that negative image might be. No, I'm talking about capable, competent career women—women who move through the world of business and finance, politics and power, as well as women who are fulfilled, accomplished, full-time homemakers.

The Lord is no respecter of persons. He is not impressed with degrees, awards, wealth, or power. Your family heritage doesn't matter. Your accomplishments and failures are not an issue with Him. It is *you* that counts with Him.

And though we can't impress Him, neither can we repel Him. He is the only one in all of life who is totally consistent and dependable. His love for all will never change no matter what we may say or do. It is unconditional.

When we allow Him to cut through our exterior façade and show us who we are, what we are, what we have done, and what He can make of us, we will never be the same. Just as with the woman at the well, all things will be new. Old fears will be lifted, and a new joy and excitement will take their place.

One day in 1970, at a point of need in my life, I very simply knelt by my bed and asked God to forgive me for all my sins and asked Jesus Christ to come into my heart and life and take over. I told Him He could have everything that I was, or could ever be, and asked Him to give me everything He had for me. And life has never been the same since that day. He gave new purpose and direction to my life.

Has it all been easy? Not at all. But He has never left me, He has always seen me through the bad times, and He has been with me in the good times. He has proven to me that there is nothing that I cannot do through Him. He is faithful, the only one you can *always* count on. And He is as real today as the sun that rises in the morning. Knowing Him is something that can't be explained; it has to be experienced.

Looking at the way Jesus treated other women in his life on earth will show even more clearly how He values women and that His mission would not have been accomplished without them. Because women were really second-class citizens in that day's culture, His manner of relating to them was revolutionary. He ignored all the old prejudices against women.

The list of women who were instrumental in the spread and development of the early church is long. First, God chose to send his only Son into the world through a woman. Men really had nothing to do with it. Men served God in many other ways, but this awesome calling came to a woman. The angel appeared to Mary—a young teen-aged girl, a virgin—and told her that she would conceive a child by the Holy Spirit. The child would be the Messiah, the Son of God. And what the angel foretold did happen. Mary and Joseph later were married, and she gave birth to the baby. Joseph served as a father to Jesus, but Mary was the key to fulfilling God's plan.

Jesus performed His first miracle at the request of a woman, His mother. He turned water into wine at the wedding feast at Cana.

Women ministered to and with Him during His three years of ministry. And another Mary sat at His feet as He taught. It was unheard-of for a rabbi to teach a woman in those days. He not only allowed Mary to sit with the men and learn; He rebuked her sister, Martha, when she asked Him to send Mary to help with the kitchen work instead.

Another time, when, as was the day's custom, the crowd wanted to stone to death a harlot taken in adultery, He had compassion. When they asked Jesus what they should do with her, He silently started writing in the sand. Many think what He wrote in the sand was a list of the sins of those in that crowd. Strangely, one by one, they dropped their stones and walked away. He then tenderly told the woman that He would not condemn her either, and to go and to sin no more.

On the road to Golgotha, called "the place of the skull," where they were taking Jesus to crucify Him, He stopped to comfort the women who stood weeping along the way. He knew these women loved Him and were hurting for Him. He loved them for that.

When Jesus looked down from the cross, and nearly all the men had run away in fear, He saw the women, the faithful women. His heart loved them for their loyalty. He said few words during that time of agony, but He did forgive his murderers. He also asked John, His friend, who was standing there by His mother, Mary, to take care of her.

Again, it was the faithful women who went to the tomb that first Easter Sunday morning to anoint the body of Jesus with spices, only to find an empty tomb. He first appeared to Mary Magdalene, one of those faithful women. And He told her that they should run and tell the Apostles—but not all the men believed them.

It can be clearly seen that Jesus did not have a condescending attitude toward women, as did the men of His day. He treated them as equals with the men, and they served as a vital part of His ministry.

It is sad that today so many women live in prisons without bars. They are in bondage to a system of their own creation, and it fails them. The women's movement, high-powered careers, modern psychology, other people—no *thing* or no *one* can truly set us free and make us whole. Only Jesus can set us free, free to be what He created us to become. There can be no greater fulfillment. You will never really know yourself until you know the God who created you in His own image.

We don't have to change words around to find or to prove our identity. If our identity hangs by such a slender thread, it will always be threatened. Calling God "She" or "Mother," as some would seek to do, doesn't change anything. God is above gender. It is just our feeble human attempt to conform God to our image, when, in exciting reality, we are created in His image. And He calls us to grow closer to Him in knowledge and relationship, so that we may be transformed by the "renewing of our minds" (Rom. 12:2), becoming more like Him. That's good news, because He is God.

Today's women are hungry and seeking, but they do not know the object of their misplaced affection. For some, the women's movement has become the false food with which they seek to feed their hungry hearts—but the hunger persists. A problem develops with the women's movement, and any other product of the world's culture, if it is committed to a self-seeking form of justice. To make life really work, we need to be committed to the Author of Justice, the true liberator.

Dr. James Kennedy, pastor of Coral Ridge Ministries of Fort Lauderdale, Florida, addresses the effect spiritual beliefs have upon society in his book *Why I Believe.* He writes:

> Christianity has brought to the world liberty and freedom. In every ancient state, the state was supreme and the individual was nothing; the individual's only significance was to serve the state. In modern times where the Gospel Christ has been banished and atheism is again regnant (as in Communist lands) the same ancient pagan doctrine is back in force. But where the Spirit of Christ is, there is liberty, and Jesus is the One who gave to the individual his worth.[2]

I had a beautiful conversation about personal liberation with
a former feminist activist who met the same Jesus that the Samaritan woman met so long ago at the well. I will call her Brenda
and with her permission I now share some of that conversation
with you.

Reflecting, Brenda said, "I think there were many things that
led me into the women's movement. My husband's work caused
him to be absent a great deal and I was forced into the role of
being both mother and father. When he came home, I would
have to back off and do things his way and on his schedule. It
was like having an occasional visitor run my life. Most of the
women I met in the women's movement had had some kind
of bad experience with men—a father, a husband, a brother,
or someone.

"I had been searching for fulfillment in all the wrong places,"
Brenda said. "I went back to school and got my degree. I thought
that was going to answer my emptiness, but that just made it
worse. Then I got a job and that didn't help either. I was ripe
for the Lord. . . ."

She then went on to tell of her conversion. "One of the things
that I wanted when I was a feminist was the power that I thought
I never had, because I felt so powerless. What the feminist movement caused me to desire was the power to control my own
life. That set me on a search for independence. I was going to
be independent economically. I was going to be independent
emotionally. I was going to be independent in every way that
I could think of, right across the board. After I became a Christian, I heard someone give an altar call that spoke to my heart
and my situation. Even though I was already a Christian, it
caused me to just sit and weep. The minister said, 'Come and
lay down your burden of independence and become dependent
on the Lord Jesus Christ.' I felt as if somebody had just taken
a weight off me, my heavy burden of independence, and I said,
'That's it. That's it. O Lord, I really didn't want to be independent; I just wanted somebody I could depend on.' Do you know
what a relief that has been for me and my husband? You see,
I always wanted from my man what only Jesus could give me—
someone who was always there when I needed him."

*It is unfair to demand or expect of spouses, careers, or accomplishments
what only God can fulfill in us.*

I felt that the saddest, most poignant thing Brenda told me that day was a conversation she had with one of her dearest friends in the feminist movement. It had taken place shortly after Brenda had committed her life to Christ. Brenda asked her friend, "I know you realize how I feel now, so can't we still be friends and just agree to disagree?"

And the friend said, "No, you have taken a path I cannot take because I know that soon you will be calling out to me for help. Jesus is just another *man* who is going to fail you."

My heart aches for Brenda's feminist friend, for she is afraid to trust. She has been hurt.

One of the beautiful things about surrendering our lives to Christ is that we develop a relationship with Him. Religions will never satisfy. They are mankind's way of seeking God through a set of beliefs. True Christianity is not a religion, but a relationship—a relationship with a person, Jesus Christ. And as He sets us free from the things of the world and from ourselves, we are no longer bound by them. Human culture can't contain us any more.

As we discover how much we are loved, our whole world changes. There is a song that says it well: "I am loved, I am loved, I can risk loving you."* That love relationship with Him allows us to lay our weapons down, for there is no longer fear of being vulnerable. For there is no *thing* or no *one* who can destroy us anymore. Our support system now is indestructible.

The fear of vulnerability, fear of not being loved, fear of not being worthy—fear of any kind—immobilizes our potential. Rebellion and pride try to deal with fear by putting down "what we fear," to exalt ourselves over it.

God's word, the Bible, tells us that perfect love casts out fear, and God's love for us is immeasurable. But first we must accept His love, through Christ.

Love is the most powerful creative force ever released upon the human soul. As the Bible tells us in 1 Corinthians 13:8, "Love never fails." Studies show that infants and baby animals die or are emotionally impaired if they are not given loving attention.

* "I Am Loved", by William J. and Gloria Gaither © Copyright 1978 by William J. Gaither. Used by permission.

God is the author of love—for He *is* love. It was love that took Christ to the cross. He would not have had to go, but He chose to go, because of His love for each of us. God is also perfect and just. His very nature cannot tolerate sin, nor can sin come into His presence through disobedience. Mankind had sinned, and for the sake of divine justice, there had to be an atonement made for that sin, or we could never come into relationship with our Creator. The wages or the result of sin is death. The only one great enough to atone for mankind's sin was God Himself. So God sent His Son, Jesus, perfect God-man, to pay that price for us. Because He shed His blood and died in our place, we can have eternal life. What kind of love is that? We can't fathom it, yet there it is! We each have, therefore, intrinsic value, which no one can take away from us.

Jesus died for us, by choice, just as we have to accept that sacrifice, by choice. His is a free gift called salvation. But like any other gift we are given, we have to receive it with an act of the will. So you see, true liberation is really a choice—our choice—to receive.

The world today offers us a well-wrapped box, all encased in shiny, polished wrapping paper tied with a lovely bow. It looks great on the outside—very appealing, neat and tidy. But, the bad news is that when we untie the bow and strip the box of its attractive wrappings, it is empty.

The free gift that Jesus offers does not disappoint us this way. His gift is eternal, always new, and precious beyond measure.

Though Jesus paid the price for all of us, He treats us individually. In an impersonal world, He calls us each, personally, by name. When God sent the angel to Mary, He called her by name. "Do not be afraid, Mary, for you have found favor with God," the angel said (Luke 1:30, NKJV). The Bible tells us that every hair on our head is numbered and that He knows when a sparrow falls from the sky.

The late Ethel Waters, a black woman, long-time entertainer and singer of popular and gospel music, was a follower of Jesus. She was renowned for her musical version of "His eye is on the sparrow and I know He watches me." About a year before her death she called my friend Mary Crowley to her. Mary and Ethel had become fast friends and Ethel called her "baby girl." Ethel took the diamond-encrusted watch from her wrist and said, "Here, baby girl, I want you to have this."

"Oh, no, Ethel, I can't take that," Mary said. "It's much too nice; you keep it."

As she pressed the watch upon Mary, Ethel broke into that warm smile so familiar to her audience. With a special twinkle in her eyes, she said, "Baby girl, I bought that in my heyday, when I made lots of money. I want you to have it. Pretty soon I'm goin' where I don't need no clock."

I am sure that the Lord she sang for those many years called her by name when, about a year later, she arrived at that place where they "don't need no clock."

In September of 1983, George Gallup, Jr., reported that 60 percent of all Americans have increasing interest in religion. He said that his survey showed "a growing conviction that religion rather than science can answer the problems of the world."

Winston Churchill, former prime minister of Great Britain, was aware that the answer to mankind's problems would not be found in science alone. He was reported as saying that we would be returning to the stone age on the gleaming wings of science.

More and more people are realizing that though we excel in science, technology, and education, so many of us fail at life. We desperately need that God who calls us by name.

> God knows you by name . . .
> God never mistakes you in the crowd.
> When a person fully realizes how
> much he or she matters to God—
> then he doesn't have to go out
> and prove to the world how
> much he matters.[3]

The Career Question

They talk about a woman's sphere
  as though it had a limit;
There's not a place in earth or heaven,
There's not a task to mankind given,
There's not a blessing or a woe,
There's not a whispered yes or no,
There's not a life, or death, or birth,
That has a feather's weight of worth—
    Without a woman in it.

Author unknown

Mary Crowley's lively eyes twinkled as she spoke in her warm Southern drawl. "Ideas can change so much," she said. "Let God have your genius. My company made $400 million in gross sales last year. They tell me, 'If ya done it, it ain't braggin'.' And we 'done it.'"

This charming, vivacious woman was at the podium, speaking in a large dining hall filled with women from the Washington, D.C., area. Included were some of the area's most influential women. She had reached the age when many women, and men, in business are thinking about retirement. Yet Mary is still going full force, and with Mary, that's saying something, for she is a human dynamo.

Since I met her five years ago, I have grown to love and admire this woman, whose heart is as big as her talent and life successes. Mary is the founder and president of Home Interiors & Gifts, Inc., headquartered in Dallas, Texas. Approximately 39,000 women across the country work for her as independent contractors.

This attractive, articulate businesswoman was sharing her life, her philosophy, and her faith at a luncheon hosted by some highly respected women in government and political circles. Her audience was comprised of women from both political parties and from all types of backgrounds. Some were professional career women in business, government, and politics. Some were wives of public officials, some were full-time homemakers, and some were part-time workers. They represented a diversity reflective of the women of this country. Mary Crowley's message that day applied to all of us in that audience, as diverse as we were.

From observing her, you might think life has always gone without struggle. That was not the case, however. She had met many challenges in her time and had started this now-booming business more than twenty-six years ago with about $6,000, a lot of prayer, and a sure vision.

The key to Mary's worldly success and her success as a human being has been her unswerving faith and commitment to her "Father." She was sharing her commitment to Christ with the women at this luncheon, as she has with so many others over the years. An inspiration and an ideal modern-day role model, Mary allows the Lord to make her faith relevant to every aspect of her personal and business life. And as Mary would say, "It works."

The reason Mary is such a good role model is because she sincerely tries to model her life after Christ and His great love for people. From the abundance with which she is blessed, she gives to many great and recognized causes—as well as to many individual humble and hurting people. I believe that is one of the reasons she continues to be blessed with such success—success for which she gives God the glory.

It was easy to see that the women in the room this bright sunny afternoon were taken with her. Mary was obviously a whole and happy woman, as well as an outstanding achiever in the world of business. And it is hard to argue with visible and true success. They listened in rapt attention to her story and the evidence of her deep-rooted faith.

Mary has never lost her humility or forgotten the importance of each individual, even though her life has so many facets. A devoted family woman as well as an astute businesswoman, she has had buildings named for her; has been recognized by United States presidents; and has been selected to serve on numerous financial, civic, and religious boards and committees. The list of honors and awards goes on and on.

She often reminds us, "People were made to be loved and things were made to be used. We get into trouble when we reverse this and begin to love things and use people." She lives by that maxim. And the love she had for singer Ethel Waters, mentioned earlier, was no greater than the love she has for the down-and-out in the inner city of Dallas, where she is involved in an outreach ministry.

Mary has lived out biblical principles in the business world, as well as in her personal life. As she trains all her new supervisors, she uses the Book of Proverbs to guide them.

Several of the thoughts expressed in the little blue inspirational book she distributes explain the attitude she relays to her saleswomen.

If you are doing more for others,
  they will be drawn to you.
If you help other people get
  what they want out of life,
You will get what you want out of life.
* * * * * * *
Help others up the ladder of
human dignity and you too will
climb upwards.
* * * * * * *
If you help someone else row
their boat across the lake—
you will reach the other shore
yourself.[1]

Those of us at the luncheon went away inspired, realizing how often we limit our own life possibilities and potential by not thinking big. Because Mary Crowley has a gift for communicating in such a direct and clear manner, I would like to include here a portion of an interview with her that appeared in the Summer 1983 issue of *Today's Christian Woman.*

TCW: One of your favorite lines is, "Be somebody because God doesn't take time to make a nobody." Why do you think so many women struggle with their self-images?
MC: I asked people in my company to write down their three basic problems in business, social situations, and home. In north, south, east, and west the main thing that came up over and over and over was lack of self-confidence—poor self-image. This just astounded me. Here we are in the greatest nation in the world, with the greatest opportunities, the highest level of education, and the most sophisticated-looking women and our problem is self-confidence.

The problem happens even among Christian women, you know. My self-confidence is tied up in the character of God, so I don't have to worry about it; and I used to think that every Christian should know that, but they don't.

She went on to explain that so much of what women see on television gives them a "fantasy" view of life and they compare themselves to that.

MC: We will never have a good self-image if we compare ourselves with somebody else. Real self-identity is seeing yourself a creature created in God's image, with his ingenuity, with tremendous potential—and not compared to anybody else; it really has to do with that inner self that God created.[2]

Mary's personal and unique approach to life is summarized in these lines from that little blue book of "quotables."

Being a Woman
One of the best things about
  being a woman is—
I don't have to go out into
  the world and prove I'm a
  man.
I speak from a full cup—
  I'm deeply glad I'm a
  woman.
I do not feel complimented
  when men say I think like
  a man.
I don't think like a man
  because I think like
  Mary Crowley.

Yes, Mary Crowley has a strong sense of personhood. Elizabeth Dole, who had taken time from her busy day at the Department of Transportation to introduce Mary at the luncheon, noted what an influence for good Mary has been in so many people's lives.

Some people do not realize how many women with prospering careers have a deep and active faith about which they speak openly. In the February 4, 1983, *Christianity Today*, Elizabeth Dole was asked in an interview: "When you addressed the National Association of Evangelicals' annual convention last year, you said you are 'shaping your work around your faith' for perhaps the first time. What does that mean?"

Elizabeth replied, "Before, my career had become all important and was sort of the center of my life. Now, my faith is central and other things flow from that. Once it is the center of your life and not an activity added to an already hectic schedule, it simplifies the complications of life that pull and push in all directions. It gives me a broader concept of how my career can be used in service to [God]. . . . I certainly see a role for the church in helping women understand what's happening and how to deal with it; accepting the problems in their lives and telling them they don't have to be all things to all people. A basic love of God and wanting his will to be done in their lives would help them work through all this."[3]

The Bible tells us that God does have a plan for our lives, as Mary emphasized when speaking to the women at the luncheon. Psalm 32:8 tells us that God will instruct and guide us in the way that we should go, and Psalm 119:105 gives us His promise to be a lamp to our feet and a light to our path. Those are just two of the many biblical promises to guide us in the plan that He has for our lives. He has a mission for us in this life, and in that path will we find fulfillment. Seeking to follow that path is seeking God's will, as Elizabeth mentioned in her interview.

Twenty years ago all of this would have sounded very strange to me, for I had no understanding at all of what it meant to give your life to Christ and seek God's will for your life. It wasn't that I would have been turned off by it, I just had no comprehension of what it was all about. I was what I would now call a "social Christian." I went to church, sometimes, because it was considered the socially "nice" thing to do, and because our families always had.

I had no idea what God thought of women, much less that He had an individual plan for my life. It has been exciting to find that God's place for women is not "second place." He may lead us into any one of a multitude of roles. And His ways are so much better than our ways. I am so grateful to have discovered that.

The views expressed about God and His plans for our lives by two women from very diverse backgrounds caught my attention in an Associated Press article by George Cornell. Justice Sandra Day O'Connor, when offered the appointment as the first woman to the Supreme Court, said, "It was like a thunderbolt. . . . I knew it would change my life unalterably and the lives of my husband, my children, parents, relatives, and friends. My first, immediate instinct was to pray to God about how to respond. The response derived from prayer was that we are to use whatever talents God has given us. I think God has a calling for each of us. . . . All of a Christian's life is under God's will. We have no right to divide our lives between time for working and time for God. We are to serve within whatever profession or trade we are in, not just outside it."

The other woman was Coretta Scott King, the widow of Dr. Martin Luther King, Jr. She stated, "In faith, you turn to the source in times of stress and there'll be direction. It may not be what you asked for, but it's what God wants you to do."

In the article, Mrs. King said that she, like O'Connor, always felt that "God has a plan and purpose for one's life and you have to pray to find it. God works through people in history to bring about justice."[4]

Reading of the tragic lives of so many today, I only wish that they knew the good news as Justice O'Connor and Mrs. King related, that there is a source we can turn to for help during life struggles. I think of an article about Brigitte Bardot in the October 1983 *People* magazine. I hurt for her as I learned of her confusion and despondency. Having had a career as a "sex symbol" in motion pictures, she now sees age taking its inevitable toll upon her beauty. She reportedly has attempted suicide a number of times and is lonely and lost. Having a great love of animals, she is said to be pouring out her love and attention upon her pets. If only she could know and receive the One who is the source of peace and of true beauty—inner beauty— the One whose love she could *count on.*

Whatever we commit ourselves to determines what we become. If we commit ourselves to the things of this world which will fade and fail, we will eventually find ourselves disappointed and empty.

There are so few who are willing to make commitments any

more—to anything that requires any effort. Current culture is oriented to instant gratification ("get it right now") and disposability ("discard it" if it isn't convenient, comfortable, or enjoyable). Unfortunately, people are often the victims of those who subscribe to these modern-day modes. If we commit ourselves to God, the author of love, then we will love people, not use them and then discard them at will.

God is more concerned about "who" we are, than "what" we do. The condition, or attitude, of our heart is the important thing. And, of course, our actions flow out of that heart condition.

Does that mean if we seek God and His goodness, we will always be right? Of course not. Because we are not perfect, we will all make mistakes. Even the best, most accomplished, and dedicated Christians make mistakes. Aren't parents more understanding when their children make honest mistakes? They respond, "I know you didn't mean it," and then go on to teach their children rather than punish them. There will be times, of course, when we simply are guilty of not doing what is right. But whatever our mistake, whether an honest mistake of omission or one of commission, our heavenly Father is an understanding and forgiving parent. There is even a bumper sticker that states that truth: "Christians aren't perfect, just forgiven."

I believe that God is more concerned about our moral attitudes than our roles. As we find our identity in Him, He will then lead us into our life roles. The dictionary defines *role* as "the proper or customary function of a person."[5] Women have been given certain biological functions and characteristics that are unique. But we are, obviously, all given different talents, gifts, and abilities, and there is a danger in limiting women within the narrow confines of a prescribed "role." I believe the Lord has many roles for us, and they may vary through the different seasons of our lives. However, in calling us to these roles, He will not violate our very nature and ignore the unique gifts He has given to us.

Someone once said that "God's plan is so simple, yet we keep missing it—first love God and then love others." That really says it all, and this is the way we are called to live, no matter what our role happens to be.

In this new era, conventions and lifestyles have changed for the many reasons discussed earlier. However, we can accommodate these new societal changes without compromising traditional values. By traditional values we mean living a life fashioned around Judeo-Christian principles, that is, loving God and loving others.

Some good things have happened because of the women's movement; I would be the last to deny that. Changes have been made that were long overdue. But in the process we have lost sight of some very important aspects of life also. The movement has focused so much upon professional career advancement, education, and governmental reforms that the role model for women that emerges from the rhetoric is still fragmented. Only one aspect of women's identity has been focused upon. The sensitive and spiritual side, which is an area of great strength and gift in women, has been all but ignored by many.

As professional career advancement has been stressed and emphasized, the roles of homemaker, wife, and mother have been devalued by default.

As educational advancement has been promoted, knowledge has been touted as providing the solutions to the questions of life. We have ignored the fact that knowledge without wisdom is useless and sometimes dangerous. Words and information flow so freely today that we are often lost in their profusion. We seem to be unaware that complexity does not guarantee certitude, but often produces confusion.

As governmental reforms have been sought, government has been projected as our source of supply and dependency, ignoring the God who created all things. Consequently, government can become a counterfeit or a substitute God.

The women's movement, while showing great concern about roles and rights, ignores the importance of building relationships. Most everyone will acknowledge that women are more "relational" than men, that is, women generally organize their lives around relationships, while men generally organize theirs around tasks. A recent Purdue University study says that girls define their friendships differently from boys; girls want someone to share their secrets with, while boys want a pal to share activities with them.[6]

As women, we need to guard our humanity. We must not become human machines. Machines can't develop relationships, nor do they have the ability to love and to give, out of caring.

Flexibility is woman's middle name as she moves from season to season in her life. Within the protective moral framework of God's laws, women should have choices in their lives, feel good about their choices, and be equipped to act responsibly upon those choices. If women are married, and especially if they have children, they must consider the high costs of a career outside the home, measuring them realistically against the benefits. Many women, of course, have been stripped of that choice through economic necessity that requires their working outside the home. I can't tell you, nor can any other person tell you, what you should do with your life. Only God knows the unique plan He has for you—and only you can seek out that plan from Him.

If you have chosen to marry, then your career decision should be made in mutual agreement with your husband. As the Lord leads you to your decision, He will work through your husband, too, and you will feel right about your choice.

We have some friends in Iowa who have worked things out to their mutual benefit. The husband told me, "We decided what works best for us. Part-time work for Bonnie is best. She keeps order in the house, and we both like it that way." Bonnie is happy with their decision, her husband is happy with it, and they have not only order, but harmony in their home. This couple is beyond the child-rearing age, their offspring married and gone. Some women enjoy staying at home and working. We should respect them for their choice. I always enjoyed working in our home, and perhaps I will work at home again someday. But this is today, and I am enjoying my present career challenges.

Some homemakers, and others who talk disparagingly about homemaking, say that housework is boring. I agree—some parts of housework *are* boring. I can tell you that *some* of the things that my position at the White House encompassed were boring also. Most jobs have some boring element about them. The grass always looks greener on the other side of the fence.

There are many things to consider when making career decisions. One important question is: how many things are we capable of keeping up with comfortably? I have a friend who says, "Some women can run a three-ring circus. Some can only run a one-ring circus. You should decide what you can run and then make your decisions."

The time spent in doing one thing obviously cannot be spent on something else. In other words, a great deal of realism is needed when married women with families make career decisions. Some women can't handle their problems at home very well, and they go into the marketplace to get away from them. Though they then have the additional salary, they still have the problems at home. Now they are just more tired when they have to face those problems.

If children are involved, there is even greater need to face career decisions realistically. Someone said to me recently, "I think the brave ones are the women who stay home and care for their children. Seeking child care for our children can be a cop-out." Of course, that is not everyone's motivation, nor is staying at home a possibility for all. Yet when mothers leave their children in the care of another, it is a decision not to be taken lightly. I can attest to the fact that the years young children are home with you go by surprisingly fast, never to be regained. Ten or fifteen years out of a lifetime is really not so long.

Mary Evelyn Blagg Huey, president of Texas Women's University, says, "It is women who have been responsible for the things that enrich our lives. It's terribly important to maintain those [things]."[7]

We women have tremendous influence, not only upon our husbands and children, but upon society, as well. We have a responsibility beyond ourselves, whether our career takes us outside the home or not. The next generation depends upon the choices women make today.

The Gift of Family

The influence of woman, the homemaker,
reaches indeed far beyond the walls of her
house. Her reach is beyond her own
comprehension. She creates the center
where the world begins, the world and all
its peoples. It is from her that they spring.
As every human being, man and woman,
emerges from her womb—and none can
otherwise be born—so they emerge from
the home she makes to receive them when
they are born. True, man is her mate and
cobuilder, but for some reason, perhaps
divine, it is she who is the more responsible
for the creation of life in all its forms.

Pearl S. Buck

How clearly I remember sitting at sunset on the back steps of our little weather-
beaten farmhouse in Iowa, listening to the crickets chirp. I would
watch alone as the long red-orange fingers of sunlight would
linger, briefly, before the glowing red disc would sink below
the gentle hills to the west of our twenty-four acre farm. Ours
was small, as farms go, even thirty-seven years ago.

There was no running water or inside plumbing, and we didn't
own the place, though we had lived there for many years and
knew it as home. It was very much a farm in spite of its small
size. We had livestock: cattle, pigs, chickens, a horse or two, a
dog, and the usual farm cats. I loved the outdoors and the animals, especially the horses. But the good things about the country
could not compensate for the loneliness I felt.

That time, at day's end, was the worst, for soon darkness
would fall, to be broken only by the flashing of the lightning
bugs that we used to catch in jars in earlier, happier days. With
the darkness, the sense of isolation always intensified.

I was thirteen and my little brother was nine. He was around,
yet it seemed as though he had neighbor friends to play with
most of the time. My mother had died just months before from
a brain tumor, which, after the surgery, the doctors said was
malignant. My father was left to share the same loneliness that
enveloped me and my brother. By day Dad worked in a factory.
After work and on weekends he worked on the farm and bought
and sold livestock to add to our income. So most of my evenings
on the back steps were spent hoping that he would be home
soon.

Though we did have electricity, there was no television in those days, nor all the other activities and attractions of today. Even if there had been, I know they would not have filled that void inside me, or been an antidote for the loneliness I felt.

Well, I survived those days of my youth, but there are still times at sunset when I find myself alone looking at that descending orb of light and experiencing the same creeping sense of loneliness from those days long gone.

In the midst of that lonely time in my life I can recall talking to a God who I believe was there, yet so far away that I was not sure He could hear me. I only wish I had known Him then. Now I know that not only could He hear me, but His loving hand was upon my life without my being aware of it. He is the one who established the family to bring individual human personalities into community with others. In Psalm 68:6 we are told, "God sets the solitary in families." Not only is community found in the humanly related family, but also in the Christian community, which the Bible calls "the family of God"—those who are spiritually related through faith in Christ.

The English journalist Malcolm Muggeridge says:

> If one can see into the meaning of nature, of happenings, and of our mortal existence, it is all incredibly beautiful. How beautiful the earth is, how beautiful is love between human beings, how wonderful is their existence in little family units which image the great family of mankind. How crazy it is that they should be ready to jeopardize that joy for trivial and worthless achievements or satisfactions.[1]

The family is the basic unit and backbone of society. Historically, when the family has disintegrated the society has fallen. The family, in spite of all its worthy attributes, is under attack today in a variety of ways. Divorce, causing the breakup of the family, is, of course, one of its most obvious foes. In that area, however, there is good news: after a pattern of increase, for the second consecutive year, the divorce rate declined in 1983.[2]

There are those radical elements within the women's movement who have targeted marriage and the family as natural enemies of women's rights and fulfillment. It is true that some husbands have not treated their wives with the respect and the fairness they are due, and that society has denied them the recognition they have earned for service. However, to label the institution of marriage and family as detrimental to the well-being of women on that basis is not only short-sighted, but villainous.

In spite of the attacks and recent criticisms of marriage and family, a survey by the American Council of Life Insurance and the Health Insurance Association of America shows that 93 percent of those surveyed believed the value of traditional family ties should be more strongly stressed.[3]

There are some who believe in the family and in traditional moral values, based upon Judeo-Christian principles, simply because they have worked in the past. They are committed to that tradition. We must be careful, though, not to replace the pursuit of truth with the pursuit of tradition for its own sake. To do so would be to ignore God, the Author of the truth upon which our moral tradition is based. It is possible to live by and benefit from God's laws without ever knowing God, for His laws applied do bring goodness and harmony. We need to be committed to God, not just His laws. Another poll reports that 68 percent of the American people in a typical twenty-four-hour period engage in one or more religious or spiritual activities.[4] It seems apparent that many anti-materialistic sentiments exist.

The Census Bureau also shows us that 73 percent of the nation's population lives in households headed by married couples. An even higher percentage would have been arrived at if an allowance has been made for unmarried young adults and elderly widows and widowers, who traditionally are more likely to live alone.[5]

Though the family is under fire by some in the secular world, I firmly believe the family will not only survive, it will flourish. For in this cold and impersonal world, which moves faster and faster, where so few things are without change, the comfort and support found in the community of the family will become increasingly prized. Most women are not going to harden themselves against the importance of family. No title, scholastic recognition, or salary check can match the inner joy of the soul when a mother hears her child say, "I love you, Mom," or her husband say, "I don't know what I would do without you, honey"— and she knows he means it.

When women come to realize that the "highest quality" life is measured in terms of human relationships rather than in terms of material things, they will begin to fully appreciate that their impact on the family has an influential effect on society as well.

The late Pearl S. Buck, Nobel Prize-winning author of many best-sellers, though a very successful career woman, had a deep appreciation for women in the home. In her book *To My Daughters, With Love*, she stated,

> Do I, who am a professional writer, believe that home-making is the most important work in the world for a woman? Yes I do, and not only for others but for myself. As a writer, I know that it is essential for a woman to be a homemaker, and this is true whatever else she is. Man and woman, we have our separate but cooperating functions to fulfill for our own completion, as well as for the human beings we serve because we are responsible for them.
>
> Woman, the housewife and homemaker, creates more than she knows. While she sweeps and cleans and makes beds, while she cooks and washes and puts away, she is creating human beings. She is shaping dispositions and building character and making harmony. The greatest need in the world today is for people of sweet disposition, and good character and tranquil, harmonious nature. . . .

It is interesting to note that, according to experts, most people are fired from jobs not because they are not doing satisfactory work, but because they can't get along with people.

Mrs. Buck adds:

> Seldom indeed do men and women rise above the atmosphere of their childhood homes. They may become rich and powerful, they may build houses very different from the one they first knew, but they carry within themselves the atmosphere of the first home. If that home was a place of order and beauty, however simple, then they are tranquil and able to cope with life's problems. If there was neither order nor beauty in the home, the lack follows them all their lives. They may not know what is the matter with them or why they are eternally restless and seeking, but they know they live in uncertainty and inner confusion.[6]

One of the greatest rewards for me as a mother, in recent years, is hearing my grown children repeat as truth some of the things I taught them long ago, things they may have disagreed with as younger children. Many of those principles I employed to train them they are now using to train their own children. The influence of mothers continues into the generations of the future.

There has been much talk in the Christian community about what the Bible has to say regarding the relationship of husband and wife in marriage. Teaching on "submission" by a few in the evangelical and fundamental church communities has at times given the impression that wives are to be the equivalent of "doormats" for their husbands to rule over. This teaching implies that wives should always stay home and never develop any of their talents and abilities. Sincere as has been the intent of this message, it has at times been overstated to the extent that some Christian women, unfortunately and incorrectly, see themselves as second-class citizens. In reality the Bible does not teach that women are to be *subordinate* to their husbands, and certainly not to all men generally; additionally, both women and men are not only bibically allowed to develop their talents, they are mandated to do so.[7]

What the Bible does teach concerning family relationships is that in the government of the family there must be one person who has ultimate authority. In God's established order of author-ity, that is the husband. It makes the wife no less important, just as Christ is no less important because He was made subject to the Father in God's order of authority (1 Cor. 11:3). Though we are to submit to one another, the wife is to willingly submit to the headship of her husband (Eph. 5:21–23). This is logical and orderly. Every successful corporation has one chief executive officer, though there is input from others before final decisions are made. Generally, in a harmonious marriage it is not very often necessary for the husband to overrule his wife in a final decision. Most decisions can be made in agreement. In fact, more often than not, the wife initiates many of the decisions that are made. Authority establishes order and harmony, when it is not abused.

The Bible gives the husband definite instructions on how to treat his wife, to love her as he would a part of himself. If both partners in a marriage follow the biblical guidelines, the relationship functions in the most satisfactory and fulfilling manner. God designed marriage, and when it is lived by his perfect plan, in his order, it is a blessing in every way to the husband, the wife, and the children.

In the February 1983 *Moody Monthly*, Sandi Frantzen wrote about women in Christian marriage.

> As a wife, she is to work alongside her husband, blessing him spiritually, physically, mentally, and emotionally.
>
> Obviously, God designed women to complement man. In the home they are to work together as partners. . . .
>
> Scripture, however, does not deny a woman her individuality or coerce her into obedience, the essence of subordination.
>
> It allows her to submit by choosing to do so. . . .
>
> As women look to the Lord Jesus Christ, they find a perfect model of willing submission to the Father. Christ's absolute submission in no way diminished his personhood. . . .
>
> But as women exercise biblical submission and as men exercise biblical headship, they will demonstrate to the world, as they work side by side, what Christ has already lived out—leadership can be conducted with compassion and sensitivity, and submission can be assumed with honor.[8]

The husband is to be the benevolent leader of the home, and husbands and wives should become one another's advocates. Some women become concerned about this order, especially if they have had domineering fathers. Such women often rebel because they fear their husbands will dominate them, as their fathers did.

Games of manipulation have no place between husbands and wives. Real love does not exploit. Trying to control a relationship by manipulation or domination only destroys intimacy. Though the husband may have the ultimate authority in marriage, there is often more power, or impact, in women's influence. Men and women are created distinctly different. Each gender is equipped to perform certain functions better than others within life, and certainly within marital relationships.

In the creation story in Genesis, woman was the completion of God's creation. God said it was not good for man to be alone, that he needed a help-mate. God did not create Eve from the dust of the earth, as He did with Adam. Rather, God drew Eve from Adam, and Adam said, "This is the bone of my bone, and flesh of my flesh. She shall be called woman, because she was taken out of man" (Gen. 2:23, ASV). I think it has great significance that the Bible says, "And God created man in his own image, in the image of God created he *him; male and female created he them* (Gen. 1:27, ASV). In Genesis 5:1–2 we are additionally told, "In the day that God created man, in the likeness of God made he *him; male* and *female* created he *them,* and blessed them, and called their name *Adam,* in the day they were created." There is no sign of inequality there: in fact, I believe that the fullness of the character of God is present when both men and women, in harmony, have developed the attributes of character with which they have been especially gifted. God Himself must have *both male and female attributes,* as we identify them, or He could not have made us *both in His image.*

We are also told in Galatians 3:28, " . . . There is neither male nor female, for you are all one in Christ Jesus." Men and women have equal spiritual worth before God.

Unfortunately, lesbianism has been encouraged by extremists in the women's movement and some promoting "sexual liberation." Some women are now seeking sexual partners of the same gender. I am sure that these relationships develop for a variety of reasons, but my Christian friend Brenda, who had been involved extensively in the feminist movement, has some interesting comments on the subject.

She said, "I knew a lot of lesbians. The ones that I knew well that were friends of mine, without exception, had either come out of bad marriages or had had an abortion. They got pregnant and the man was not willing to take the responsibility. Or they had some kind of bad association with a man and there was distrust. So, economically, what happened is that sometimes these women would begin to live together because they couldn't handle it financially. What began as caring and nurturing of one another became a lesbian relationship. I am sure there are other kinds of situations that occur, but with the people I knew personally, that is how it evolved in every one of the cases."

It is true all of us have a need to be loved, valued, and have someone with whom we can be intimate in our lives. In the case of lesbianism, women are trying to meet their own needs without the threatening element of a man in the relationship, a man who, they fear, would control that relationship. It is sad, for it is not the highest quality of life.

Lesbianism and homosexuality are biologically, medically, and biblically a perversion. Biologically, reason and logic alone state loudly that two members of the same gender do not complement one another. These same sex practices would lead to the extinction of the human race if followed by all. Medically, evidence continually grows that physical and emotional danger of disease and illness abound in these relationships. Biblically, there is no room left for doubt or confusion about the moral acceptability of this lifestyle. It, very simply, is called sin. However, Jesus did not come to condemn, but to forgive and make whole. He loves us all and died for all of humanity—for all of us sinners.

In an article in the *Miami Herald*, Colin Cook, who has a ministry to homosexuals, says homosexuality

> is a search for completeness. . . . It's a search that continues until the person finds his identity, which is based ultimately on a relationship with Jesus Christ and the Heavenly Father. It's a same-sex, but not an erotic, relationship. Once this relationship is formed, the erotic need for the same sex begins to diminish. . . . God's grace accepts people who struggle with homosexuality and helps them through it.[9]

In normal heterosexual relationships, women have been gifted with the unique ability to become mothers. Women have nurturing and nesting instincts. It is a natural thing for women to desire to make a home. Though money buys a house, women make a home, and there is a vast difference. Women bring quality to life.

As more and more women have entered the marketplace and the women's movement has stressed pursuing out-of-the-home careers, mothers are faced with the dilemma of whether to leave their children. One woman, telling me of her personal decision to stay home with her children, said, "What working mothers leave is not just an empty house, but lonely children."

Presently, nearly two-thirds of the mothers with children older than six have left the home to enter the work force. I believe that most of us would agree that in each heart there is one special corner that only a mom can fill. Responsibility requires that some of the negative results of mothers working be honestly assessed. Numerous articles have been written about the loss of the age of innocence for children today. Many of America's children no longer have a childhood, because many are required at a young age to meet adult responsibilities and care for themselves.

Ron and Lynette Long, co-authors of *The Handbook for Latchkey Children and Their Parents,* estimate that in this country there may be as many as fifteen million children left routinely unattended for some period most days. Latchkey children are children who unlock and enter an empty house everyday in their working parents' absence. The Longs found in their interviews of former latchkey children that more than half felt there was some negative carry-over.[10]

The fact that suicide has been the third leading cause of death among teenagers should give adults cause for great concern. Loneliness and the feeling of those teenagers that no one cares or understands their problems contribute to the despondency of many.

I came across some interesting and thought-provoking statements in a recent newspaper. Steven Stack of Pennsylvania State University expressed the opinion that religion supplies moral guidelines, and that young people, while freer, "are more unhappy." Child psychologist David Elkind said, "Today's child has become the unwilling, unintended victim of overwhelming stress born of rapid, bewildering social change and constantly rising expectations." The message received from the young by Dr. Donald McKnew of the National Institute of Mental Health is that they're "not very happy," and that it is "because of their parents."

Another factor to be noted is the finding of a recent study conducted jointly by the Department of Education and Decision Resources that children from one-parent families, or children from two-parent families whose mothers work, tend to have lower academic achievement.[11]

These are not necessarily pleasant considerations; however, as a society and as parents, we have a responsibility to acknowledge and consider them.

In this day of the working mother, we hear a great deal about "quality time." Dr. James Dobson, an associate clinical professor at the University of Southern California School of Medicine, and a greatly respected author and family counselor, has some interesting and worthwhile observations on this subject. When

asked if quality time is not more important than quantity time
with our children, he replied:

> There is a grain of truth in most popular notions, and this one
> is no exception. We can all agree that there is no benefit in being
> with our children seven days a week if we are angry, oppressive,
> unnurturing and capricious with them. But from that point for-
> ward, the quantity versus the quality issue runs aground. Simply
> stated, that dichotomy will not be tolerated in any other area of
> our lives: why do we apply it only to children? Let me illustrate.
> Let's suppose you are very hungry, having eaten nothing all
> day. You select the best restaurant in your city and ask the waiter
> for the finest steak on his menu. He replies that the filet mignon
> is the house favorite, and you order it charcoal-broiled, medium
> rare. The waiter returns twenty minutes later with the fare and
> sets it before you. There in the center of a large plate is a lonely
> piece of meat, one inch square, flanked by a single bit of potato.
> You complain vigorously to the waiter, "Is this what you call
> a steak dinner?"
> He then replies, "Sir, how can you criticize us before you taste
> that meat? I have brought you one square inch of the finest steak
> money can buy. It is cooked to perfection, salted with care, and
> served, while hot. In fact, I doubt if you could get a better piece
> of meat anywhere in the city. I'll admit that the serving is small,
> but after all, sir, everyone knows that it isn't the quantity that
> matters: it's the quality that counts in steak dinners."
> "Nonsense!" you reply, and I certainly agree. You see, the sub-
> tlety of this simple phrase is that it puts two necessary virtues
> in opposition to one another and invites us to choose between
> them. If quantity and quality are worthwhile ingredients in family
> relationships, then why not give our kids both? It is insufficient
> to toss our "hungry" children an occasional bite of steak, even
> if it is prime, corn-fed filet mignon.
> Without meaning any disrespect to you for asking this question,
> my concern is that the quantity-versus-quality cliché has become,
> perhaps, a rationalization for giving our kids neither! This phrase
> has been bandied about for overcommitted and harassed parents
> who feel guilty about the lack of time they spend with their chil-
> dren. Their boys and girls are parked at child care centers during
> the day and with baby-sitters at night, leaving little time for tradi-
> tional parenting activities. And to handle the discomfort of neglect-
> ing their children, Mom and Dad cling to a catch phrase that
> makes it seem so healthy and proper: "Well, you know, it's not

the quantity of time that matters, it's the quality of your together-ness that counts." I maintain that this convenient generalization simply won't hold water.[12]

The question that modern-day mothers have to ask themselves is, what price are my children paying for my lifestyle? If mother is working to add to the family income to raise the standard of living, she and her husband must weigh that "high-cost family living" against the true cost of that "high living." Is the price too great?

Even if mothers do not work outside the home, the effect of their lifestyle on their children must be assessed. As mothers, encouraged by society, have become more efficient, sometimes something is lost. In rushing here and there, marketing, shopping, carpooling, and so on, that something could be the precious time for just "mothering," the time to develop the bonds of relationship with children. We need to take time to make memories. As poet May Riley Smith said so beautifully, "Strange we never prize the music till the sweet-voiced bird has flown. . . ."[13]

A young woman who left her full-time job as a linguist when her second son was born writes, "I have to be around my chil-dren—a lot. I have to know them as well as I possibly can and see them in as many different environments and moods as possi-ble in order to know best how to help them grow up, by comfort-ing them, letting them alone, disciplining and enjoying them. What I need with them is time—in quantity, not quality."[14]

Why do mothers have children, if they then turn around and place them in the care of others for the greatest share of the time? Children need their mothers. Children need *time* with their mothers. The bonding and emotional ties that develop between them affect children's personalities, attitudes, and values—greatly influencing the shaping of their character. If we have a choice, do we really want to entrust that influence to others?

In no way do I intend here to overlook or downgrade the influence of fathers upon their children. Neither do I intend to indicate that it is not desirable for fathers to take a greater share in the care and raising of their children. They should. Fathers have a role of great importance, also. However, no matter how we may try to intellectualize the fact away, a mother's impact upon her child's development is of paramount consequence. Women carry and bear children. Women become "mothers" as they love and nurture those children through their formative years.

The joys of motherhood more than compensate for the sacrifices. Motherhood also builds character. In sacrifice, freely given, mothers stay up nights with sick children, put on and pull off winter clothes, change diapers and wipe runny noses, all the while developing patience, perseverance, and a strength that is of great benefit when applied in any other life situations. Mothers lay down their lives for their children out of love. I believe the denigrating of motherhood, in recent times, is self-deception, an attempt to camouflage selfishness. Not only children, but women and society are the losers.

We reap what we sow. Is it any wonder that many of today's children are confused and lonely, lost and frightened? The security that comes from realizing that your parents love you and that there is hope for the future is missing for many. When your parents—or any other person—are willing to give you, not just their things, but their time, it speaks loudly of their love for you.

In this nuclear age in which children are growing up today, with its fear of worldly destruction, there is a desperate need for hope. Not just children, but all of us need hope in something beyond ourselves, something beyond this earthly life. The *only* place that hope can be found is in faith in the God who created the universe.

Sadly, this hope-producing faith in God often is lacking in modern parents' lives, or is not communicated by them to their children. For years, this faith was traditionally learned by children at their mother's knee.

I have often heard President Reagan speak of his mother, the late Nelle Reagan, an unassuming, little-known woman, who had an influence far beyond her years here on this earth. Her son, the president of the United States, swore his oath of office with his hand upon her worn Bible—a Bible with verses underlined and notes in its margins. Nelle Reagan's son is today shaping public policy that affects not only this country but the world. And many of his judgments are based upon the faith and value system she imparted to him more than seventy years ago. Now that is influence! She never received any public recognition for her efforts, but then she didn't do it for recognition—she did it for love.

The effect of a loving mother on her child is portrayed clearly by the following poem, author unknown.

MOLDING LIFE

I took a piece of plastic clay
And idly fashioned it one day;
And as my fingers pressed it still,
It moved, and yielded to my will.

I came again when the days were past;
The bit of clay was hard at last;
The form I gave it still it bore,
But I could change that form no more.

I took a piece of living clay,
And gently formed it day by day,
And molded with my power and art
A young child's soft and yielding heart.

I came again when the years were gone,
It was a man I looked upon;
He still that early impress wore
And I could change him nevermore.[15]

The influence of a loving mother has had a tremendous impact upon many of the world's leaders. It would be revealing to study the lives of the mothers of some of our presidents and their relationship with their children. It is public knowledge that the late Lillian Carter had a strong influence on her son, former President Jimmy Carter. And in one of his life's darkest moments, President Nixon, as he was resigning the presidency under a cloud, spoke of his mother. He called her "a saint." He may well have been reaching back for some of the spiritual strength he knew she possessed—a pain-filled tribute to a loving mother.

Love takes commitment, and commitment does mean sacrifice. Commitment to another person costs us some of self, but the rewards are very great.

I was fortunate enough to have been present when the Rossow family from Connecticut came to the White House at the invitation of President Reagan. He had seen their unusual family story related on a television program and was captivated by the selflessness of this loving couple, who had fourteen children. Eleven of them were adopted, and all of the eleven were severely handicapped. As they arrived at the Roosevelt Room across from the Oval Office that afternoon, nine of the children were in wheelchairs. It would take pages to describe their deformities, for they were varied and extensive. Suffice it to say here that to care for them must be an enormous task. The youngest child, a boy named Benjy, was a year and a half old. Benjy was born with an affliction that prevents the brain from developing. He cannot see, speak, or walk, and he never will. As the family assembled in the room to await the president and Mrs. Reagan, those of us present were struck by the love emanating from this couple, the parents. It was obvious that their love and encouragement was the only thing that kept some of these children going.

President and Mrs. Reagan entered the room to meet and to talk with all the children, as the parents gave the Reagans a little background on each child. One of the children then played a tape recording of a nun playing a guitar and singing a song that she had written called "Benjy." In the song she so poignantly described the love this young child brought to those around him, even though he could not communicate. It was moving, indeed, and Mrs. Reagan had to turn her back to the press as the tears ran down her cheeks. Then in one of the most insensitive displays of aggressive journalism I ever witnessed, a woman reporter asked in a sarcastic voice, "Mr. President, what are you trying to tell us here? What does this mean?"

With greater patience than I would have possessed, the president replied, with a catch in his voice, "The Bible says that we should love our neighbor. And this is the greatest example of love I've ever witnessed." There was silence and the reporter said no more.

Love within the family is precious. It has no price tag, for it is beyond price. The Rossow family was a beautiful example of "family love." Every family has the potential for that kind of love. Sadly, it is undeveloped or left uncommunicated in some families.

As a mother, through your relationship with your children, you see your life reproduced in another as you train them, mold them, transmit your values to them. A recent newspaper article told the story of a career woman in her thirties who, after having her first child, said, "I planned to go back into work immediately." As her child began to grow, she confessed, "Tremendous affection took over. In that three- or four-month period, a child really becomes a human being and it's very difficult to leave them. It didn't make sense for me to go through all of this to give her to someone else to raise."[16]

It is true, marriage and motherhood do bring God-given distractions from self, calling us to give for the sake of others, but we receive as we give. In the family, solitary individuals can be bound together by love into community and into nurturing relationships. Within the family unit, if we are willing to give freely and fully for the sake of the other members, the family can be a "cocoon of love" in which individuals grow, develop, find fulfillment—and then go out into the world from that supportive environment. Loving relationships not only sustain us in life but affect us in death. For when that time comes for each of us to leave this world, as it surely will, what will matter will not be the power we acquired, the money we made, or the honors we received. What will matter will be relationships. First, what is our relationship to the God to whom we will return? Then, what is our relationship to our family, to our friends, and, yes, to our enemies?

The Seasons of Life

God's plan, like lilies
   pure and white, unfolds.
We must not tear the close-shut
   leaves apart.
Time will reveal the calyxes
   of gold.

May Riley Smith

The woman who came through the door into my office was a friend I had not seen for many years. (I'll refer to her here as Ginny.) Her countenance was not what I had expected. I realized that the years have a way of taking their physical toll, but there was something more devastating than age that had extracted a price from my old friend. The lines around her eyes, the creases in her forehead, the tightness of her mouth, all spoke of pain. Trying not to show my shock, I directed her to the couch and sat next to her, saying how great it was to see her.

Ginny had told my secretary she was in town on business and wanted just a few minutes to drop by my White House office. Her voice quivered as she told me how pleased she was to see where I was working and to know I was doing well. Sensing that something drastic had gone wrong in her life, I quickly reflected on the Ginny I had known in days gone by. She had been one of those people who would come to mind when you thought of civic "doers"—active in everything, and very well thought of in her local community. Ginny had a good education, a successful husband, a fine family, a lovely home, and high social standing—all the criteria for success by society's standards.

Looking straight into her eyes, I asked the question that opened the floodgates. "How are you, Ginny?"

Barely contained tears now burst forth and streamed down her face. She said, "Oh, Dee, I'm terrible!"

I encouraged her to tell me what had happened, and she revealed that her husband had left her for someone else; there had been a terrible court battle over finances, and somehow or other she had come out very poorly. Her children were now grown and gone; she could not afford the big, beautiful, empty house; and all the years of giving her time and talents to the community were no help in her search for a job. She had no salaried work history to speak of, and she was about fifty years old. Most firms are not eager to hire someone of that age.

As Ginny talked, I could see that something even more devastating had happened to her. This former proud, self-confident, well-respected community leader's self-esteem had been ground into fine powder. As she spoke of her struggles and inability to get her life together, her lack of confidence and sense of defeat colored each sentence. I felt such great compassion for her, yet wasn't sure what I could do to help, except hug her.

Reassuring Ginny of her ability and worth, I made several suggestions about employment. Then Ginny, knowing it was a source of strength in my life, asked about my faith. This was a hurting human being who needed strength beyond herself.

In the months that followed, I kept in touch with her, and things did get better for her. She found a position, her frazzled nerves began to heal, and, most important, she drew close to the God who loves her—the only One, she came to realize, that we can *always* count on for unconditional love. God used her "hurts" to draw her to Himself, strengthening her in those times of trial, which became times of growth.

Ginny has now moved into a "new season" in her life, in which I am sure there will be exciting and unexpected rewards. As the well-known passage in Ecclesiastes 3:1 says, "For all things there is a season, and a time for every purpose under heaven. . . ."

The things of our childhood are not the things for the time of our maturity, and when we do not deal with the proper things in their season, problems result. But change is not easy; indeed, often it is quite painful. And, of course, fear is an enemy which can cause us to fight rightful change, instead of flowing with it.

God does have a plan for our lives, a plan that will be for His glory and for our ultimate good. Let's not fight life and miss the gentle guiding hand of the Father as we traverse the

changing terrain of our journey. To do that is to live life with
an ever-present riddle that will still be without answer when
we whisper our last breath.

In *Growing Strong in the Seasons of Life*, Charles R. Swindoll writes,

> As each three-month segment of every year holds its own myster-
> ies and plays its own melodies, offering sights and smell, feelings
> and fantasies altogether distinct, so it is in the seasons of life.
> The Master is neither mute nor careless as He alters our times
> and changes our seasons. How wrong to trudge blindly and rou-
> tinely through a lifetime of changing seasons without discovering
> answers to the new mysteries and learning to sing the new melo-
> dies! Seasons are designed to deepen us, to instruct us in the wis-
> dom and ways of our God. To help us grow strong . . . like a
> tree planted by the rivers of water.

Swindoll goes on to encourage us to "read God's signals with
a sensitive heart."[1]

Yes, there are many seasons in our lives, and what is good
for us at twenty-five truly wouldn't be good for us at forty-
five. Perhaps, after working for a brief season—one, two, or
more years—then marrying and having children, a woman may
choose to stay home for a longer season and raise her family.
At that point in life there may be another twenty-year season
to devote to a second career, if she chooses, before entering a
season of retirement.

This time is a new season in my personal life, as I reach age
fifty. I am no longer the young farm girl, or the single parent,
or a wife and the mother to six growing children. Now I am
grandmother to five and an active career woman.

To those people who say, "Oh, I would give anything to be
eighteen again!" I reply, "Not me." I wouldn't go back a year,
and I look forward to what lies ahead. I believe God has something special and exciting in each season, if we will expectantly
walk in it. God is never to be limited.

When my husband was elected to the United States Senate
in 1978 and we moved to Washington, we moved into a new
season in our lives. But I came very close to fighting God's timing
and His new season for me. Now I am grateful I did not.

As I mentioned earlier, when my husband was in public office years ago, we had some difficult times, as the demands and beck-onings of that life took its toll on our relationship. It was then that I committed my life to Christ and started on life's journey with a new perspective. My husband came to that same life commitment some years later, after leaving political life—forever, so I thought.

My memories of political life were not good and I was thankful that it was behind us. I thought it threatened everything that I really cared about the most—marriage, family, relationships. Although I was pleased that public life was over, I never stopped promising the Lord He could do anything with me that He wanted, never dreaming, of course, that politics might be in-volved in our future.

When my husband mentioned that he was considering running for the U.S. Senate, I thought my heart would stop. My world seemed shattered. It was a time of great personal inner struggle for me—and much prayer and conversation between Roger and me. I was hesitant, to say the least, but if I had not been willing to step out into the unknown, toward what I feared the most, I would have missed a new and rewarding season the Lord had for me. It would have not only closed doors for me, but for my husband. I was nearly that timid and selfish. I thank God that He was patient and merciful to me.

Helen Keller, the late blind and deaf author, wrote, "When one door of happiness closes, another opens; but often we look so long at the closed door that we do not see the one which has been opened for us."[2]

The irony is that God used the very thing I feared and disliked the most and turned it into a blessing in my life, in my personal life and in our marriage. Public life, politics, which had been a wedge between us before, now has drawn us closer together. Strange how God can turn negatives into positives, if we will just yield our wills and give Him a free hand to work in our lives.

Yes, coming to Washington was truly a "new season" for me, in many ways. I had never really lived anywhere but in my hometown. I had not worked outside our home for twenty years, other than as a volunteer and briefly in the small business I co-founded. In the fall of 1978 our last child left home for college. The children were all on their own and my time was without other demands upon it, so Roger and I could work together. The timing was right; it all fit together.

It has all worked out so well now that it dulls the memory of the changes by which I felt threatened at that time of crucial decision. But it meant that I must be willing, if we won the election, to leave the familiar and comfortable hometown of a lifetime. I would also have to leave my children and all my family in the area, the big attractive home I had decorated with my own hands, and loved, and all my friends—in other words, my roots. I was releasing all that to walk toward that thing I most feared. Yet the Lord builds trust like that, by stretching our faith and teaching us to trust Him with our lives. Whenever I tell that story I always hasten to add that I do not tell it for political reasons, but rather to give glory to God for His loving care. He has truly guided me to growth through the seasons of our lives.

Before we can walk through the seasons of our lives with a heart sensitive to what Swindoll calls "God's signals," we must come into relationship with Him. It requires an act of our will that opens the door of our hearts to His son, Jesus, for He won't force Himself on us. We have free choice to accept or reject Him. It has been said that the greatest and most important question of life is, "What will you do with Jesus Christ?"

If we choose to accept Him and the gift of salvation He freely offers to us, then things start to change. Will the circumstances of our lives become better immediately? Probably not. I know mine certainly didn't when I made that decision. But *we* start to change in the midst of our circumstances. Sometimes the changes are drastic and sometimes subtle, but change we will. And it is a change we can't put on from the outside.

Gordon Jensen's popular song says,

> Inside out
> That's what this change is
> all about.
> . . . .
> It's not something you can
> do on your own
> That we're talking about.
> It's not struggling to do

What's impossible for you.
But it's Jesus' love
   changing you
From the inside out.*

It is change in the most radical sense, becoming as new. As this change takes place, we will find that we are at peace, not only with our God, but with ourselves and our neighbors—for we have met the Prince of Peace.

We will become aware of a new self-esteem as we realize God's love for us. We will start esteeming others as we discover that God loves everyone else just as much as He loves us. We will recognize that Christ died on the cross for every one of us. It doesn't matter what our station in life may be; that has no bearing on our spiritual worth. Nor does it matter how unlovable we may be. In God's book we all have intrinsic value; we all have equal spiritual worth. *No one* or *no thing* can take our worth from us. When we understand our value to the Creator God, we will realize that.

Driving up to those big iron gates to enter the parking area at the White House each morning, I had to pass some of the "street people" who sleep on the steam grates in the city's parks. The same ragged people can be found in the same place for years. Many will not leave their spot, for it is home to them. Even when the snow is deep and the winds are cold, they often refuse shelter. In my daily drive to work, the thought often came to me that our God loves them just as much as He loves the man I worked for in the White House across the street. The ground at the foot of the cross is truly level.

A Christian friend said something interesting to me one day when we were discussing the importance of women and the ongoing debate about women's issues. She said, "You know, men and women are both here for the same reason—to serve each other." I had never thought of it just like that, but it is true. If we were truly to live by the Golden Rule and "do unto others as you would have them do unto you," that is what we would do—serve each other.

Service is considered out of vogue, however, by some people today. I must admit that came as something of a surprise to me, having said so often that "it is a noble thing, to have a heart of a servant." I believe it to be true. And service used to be universally recognized in the business world as something important to be developed; it was a maxim that when you give good service you reap rewards in business success. And of course, the Bible teaches that when we give, we receive. Anyone who has ever given, by choice, to another in need, knows that deep feeling of satisfaction at having brought pleasure to another.

One day in an interview I made the statement that it was a noble thing to have a heart of a servant, and I was quoted in the newspaper. The next day one of the well-known business news publications ran an item repeating the quote, with the added tongue-in-cheek put-down, "Fetch us a Coke, Dee." The quote also appeared, attributed to me, in a contemporary women's magazine. It was in an article composed of two parallel columns. One was captioned, "Sounds like an old lady," and the other caption read, "Sounds like a new woman." My quote was relegated to "Sounds like an old lady."

I had added in that interview that women are very good at serving. It is a fact that women have always stepped forward to serve when there were needs to be met, not only in the home but in the community, and for the sake of the country, in times of war and crisis. And no matter how much anyone may *think* serving is "old-fashioned," its value will never be outdated.

I was touched by a conversation with a Catholic priest who had returned to the States briefly from a mission to the Indians in the Bolivian Andes Mountains. "Father Willie" was telling about the utter poverty of the people, the disease, the poor hygiene, the huts with dirt floors. Looking at me with tender eyes, which revealed the gentle compassionate heart of the man, the priest said, "Serving is a wonderful way to be human." His role model was the greatest servant of all, Jesus.

I hope that I never forget that, for it so easy to get caught up in ourselves and miss the many opportunities around us to be a blessing to others.

There is something paradoxically attractive about freely giving of ourselves. For life is divided into two parts—the natural or worldly, and the spiritual. And just as there are natural principles, there are spiritual principles. It is a spiritual principle that "in giving, we receive." The call to serve is a spiritual call, to rise above the selfishness of our human nature, a call to set "self" aside for the benefit of others.

Why did the closing words of President John F. Kennedy's Inaugural Address in 1961, "Ask not what your country can do for you; rather, ask what you can do for your country," capture the imagination of the nation? That stirring challenge ignited in the hearts of Americans the desire to push for higher ground. It inspired in us a vision of greatness, a vision of what we could become. It spoke of a president's belief in a people. It made us feel good about ourselves.

There is a part of us that wants to be reminded that we can do better, that we can ascend to a new high standard, that we can overcome a lesser life. Some would say, "But that is to ignore things as they really are. That is not reality." I would remind that we don't hold up mediocrity as a goal toward which to strive. Mediocrity comes without much effort.

One of the problems created by some of the leaders in the women's movement is the focus on "getting" to the exclusion of "giving"—the demand for rights and recognition, the push for position and power. While some of the goals sought may be fair and just, if we turn totally in upon ourselves, we become sick with introspection. We become like "dead seas," stagnant and unable to support real life.

Of course, we do not have to be involved in the women's movement or any other cause to get so caught up in our own lives and interests that we become self-centered. We all slip into that state so easily.

In speaking to gatherings of women my age and older who are entering the fall and winter seasons of their lives, I have often thought what a valuable resource they are. They are a veritable pool of talent waiting to be tapped. With the longer life expectancy we enjoy today, there are millions of older women who have good health and no major family responsibilities, leaving them with the time, as well as the talent, to do so many things with their lives. For the first time in the history of this country, we have more Americans age sixty-five and older than we have teenagers. Let's not put them on the shelf, but rather encourage and allow them to use their skills to help others, renewing their own vitality in the process.

Many women, and men, in their middle and later years, have made tremendous contributions to their communities. However, there are also some who could be called "seekers of positive pleasure." Recreation, of course, is healthy. Some people today, however, have slipped into a lifestyle centered upon merely seeking innocent ways in which to entertain themselves. This is especially true of some women in their late forties and fifties. But how much better life would be, for themselves and for those whom their service could help, if they were to give some of their time and their many talents toward serving. After the daily struggles of raising a young family were past, I considered what would be the best way to spend my time. The passage from 1 Corinthians 7:31 spoke to me about how to approach the world: "And those who deal with this world—overusing the enjoyments of this life—let them live as though they were not absorbed by it, and as if they had no dealings with it. For the outward form of this world—the present world order—is passing away."

Sometimes all it takes to get people activated is for someone to remind them how much they really have to offer and how many people out there could benefit from their abilities. Some of today's problems could be solved if each of us took it upon ourselves to help someone else, even in a very small, "everyday" way. They would be helped, we would be helped, and the spirit of our country would improve.

A letter I received from a gentleman in Virginia last year exemplified this kind of giving spirit. He wrote after hearing me discuss volunteerism on a radio talk show when I was serving on the President's Task Force for Private Sector Initiatives. The letter was printed in a very shaky hand and someone had typed the words below his message. After some complimentary opening remarks and the information that he was a Christian, he said, "Since I am a person who is legally blind I assure you I know something about loneliness and the struggle to hang in there." He enclosed a poem and a poster for me about "hanging in there" even when the going was tough.

He went on, "During the past ten years I have been involved in presenting a program entitled 'Reaching in, Reaching out, and a Helping Hand' to a wide variety of groups, including adults and youth. It has been an enriching experience and has enabled me to maintain my self-image and remain in the mainstream of society. I am still going strong at seventy-three years young."

I say "hip, hip, hurray" for that special child of the Lord!

To give and serve no matter what our season of life, whether we are in the home or out of the home, is a calling we all share. If we have come to know the God who loves us, sharing His love with others is a privilege.

A story Senator Mark Hatfield tells about Mother Teresa illustrates this loving, serving spirit. Senator Hatfield was visiting her and had toured her Home for the Destitute and Dying in Calcutta, India. After seeing the suffering and smelling the stench of death, he turned to the tiny woman and asked, "Mother, how can you continue to do this, in the face of such abject poverty? You know you can't make a dent in things."

With that inner glow that always lights her face, this selfless servant said, "Senator, God didn't call me to be successful; He called me to be faithful." She was doing what her God would have her do. Her call was to obedience and service.

Poet Barbara Burrow so well describes the successful woman who used her talents to serve through all the various seasons of her life.

> That woman is a success . . .
>
> who loves life
> and lives it to the fullest;
> who has discovered and shared
> the strengths and talents
> that are uniquely her own;
> who puts her best into each task
> and leaves each situation
> better than she found it;
> who seeks and finds
> that which is beautiful
> in all people . . . and all things;
> whose heart is full of love
> and warm with compassion;
> who has found joy in living
> and peace within herself.[3]

Life-Bearing:
Blessing or Burden?

You made all the delicate, inner parts of
my body, and knit them together in my
mother's womb. Thank you for making me
so wonderfully complex! It is amazing to
think about. Your workmanship is
marvelous—and how well I know it. You
were there while I was being formed in utter
seclusion! You saw me before I was born
and scheduled each day of my life before
I began to breathe. Every day was recorded
in your Book!

Psalm 139:13–16, TLB

It was dawn. The sun was just flirting with the sky, visible through the window of her room. She couldn't be sure just what time it was because her watch was in the drawer of the night stand and she couldn't reach it. As Ann tried to collect her thoughts, the full realization of what had happened hours before swept over her. She had had her baby—a little girl! They would name her Tiffany. Michael liked that name. And he was such a proud father. She could remember that, although the events of last night were still a little fuzzy.

Now she knew what had awakened her. From down the corridor of the hospital's maternity ward, breaking the quiet of the early morning, came that unmistakable sound—the cry of newborn babies, that irregular throaty rattle emanating from newly tried lungs. As the soft padding of a nurse's shoes on the polished floor of the hall drew near her room, Ann knew that she must be bringing her baby to her.

Switching on the soft light above Ann's bed, the nurse said, "Good morning, Mother Gregory. Here's your baby."

How wonderful that sounded! Ann reached out and took the little bundle. Those last months had been filled with questions for her. Would it be a boy, or a girl? What would this baby look like? Would it have blond hair like Michael's or dark hair like hers? But most of all, would the baby be all right? She prayed it would.

Ann could hardly draw her eyes away from that precious little one long enough to give attention to the nurse's instructions about feeding the hungry baby.

Finally, the nurse left. Ann was glad that the other bed in the room was empty, as now mother and baby were alone. She gazed lovingly down at this little girl, *her* little girl, and was filled with a quiet awe. As she kissed the soft, silky skin of the baby's pink forehead, the smell of baby blending with the fragrance of powder, oil, and freshly washed flannel greeted her nose. That special smell of a new baby was better than perfume, she thought.

Oh, how beautiful she was—so tiny, so fragile. Yet perfect, Ann could see, as she unwrapped the tightly bound blanket, counting and inspecting the teeny fingers and toes. "Oh, thank you, God," she whispered. "She's perfect."

Ann knew she would always treasure the memory of this moment spent with this new life, this new person—her baby. Tears of joy filled her eyes as they met the eyes of her little girl, as the baby squinted up into the face of her mother for the first time—on this, the first day of life outside the womb.

As Ann looked at this newborn, she realized the impact which she would have upon this essentially blank human slate. She recognized that, as the character, personality, values and attitudes of this new life were shaped, she would place her lasting imprint upon them—an imprint that would carry into future generations. The wonder of it all!

An article that appeared in the *Washington Post* early in 1984 gave vent to feelings in sharp contrast to those of the new mother in the scene just described. The author of the article declared that the women's revolution in the United States was only "half won." She called the "burdens" of child-rearing a "serious obstacle" to women's being able to take advantage of the new opportunities that are now open to them.[1]

All human life upon this earth comes into it through women. Life-bearing is the indisputably unique characteristic of woman. Woman is created with the undeniable ability to bear children. Women are the "mothers" of the world, and no amount of legislation, complaints, or societal attitude conditioning can change that. It is fact, it is truth—like it or not.

Is it a blessing, or is it a burden? Is it all a divine mistake—this mission in life? Many of today's reverberating "voices" have given rise to questions like these within the hearts of America's "today" women. The questions have perhaps been unacknowledged, or have remained but vague stirrings—thoughts not yet clothed with words. But they are there all the same.

I am reminded of the many discussions I have had with women, and men, over the last six years about the volatile issue that is a natural result of today's social and moral strugglings—abortion. One such conversation took place in a meeting in my husband's Senate office while I was still volunteering full time there.

Roger's schedule did not permit him to meet with a group of Iowans who were stopping by his office, while visiting Washington, that day. I met with them so I could later convey to him their message. They wanted to discuss an effort that was close to their hearts. I knew several people in the group, having worked with them in some civic activities and community causes in their home area in the past. They were fine, responsible citizens, contributing their time and talent to their community in many ways. Besides all of that, I liked them very much as human beings. What they had on their minds that day was to discuss the problems involved in teenage pregnancy, a problem about which all society should share concern. One of the available and acceptable options in case of such a pregnancy, in their view, should be abortion.

I do not share that view, nor does my husband. Though the problem of pregnancy among unwed teenage girls is traumatic and tragic, abortion compounds the tragedy and is not a morally acceptable solution.

As I attempted to explain to them why I held that view, I found myself so wishing they could comprehend the profound wrong of abortion. I knew their hearts were right, and that their goal was to help young girls who were in desperate need. Theirs was a pragmatic solution, presented in an attempt to solve one of the many problems that plagues modern society. I felt sure their acceptance of abortion was based upon a false presumption. That presumption was that unborn babies are not unborn babies, but rather, something other than human life. I simply do not believe that. Is it not a society with a deeper problem that seeks to solve some of its social problems by eliminating its young— embracing an ethic of human disposability?

Abortion is an intensely emotional issue, and feelings run deep on both sides of the question.

In the months following that meeting, I met with many people who also supported abortion, but for another reason. Many of them sincerely believed that they were supporting and working for a moral cause, as they sought to defend the right of women to choose whether to have abortions or not. They call their cause "pro-choice." Pro-choice advocates believe that women should be insured the right to make a free choice about abortion, thus having the right to control their own bodies. Though I do not agree, I understand the premise of their argument and do not condemn them.

To all those who support abortion, however, based upon what they see as humane problem-solving or rightly motivated reasons, I must issue an urgent appeal: Take another look at this serious question. What you are doing is similar to making the seemingly small, yet potentially fatal, decision about crossing a street, after having looked in only one direction. Had I looked in only that one direction, perhaps I would have agreed with the decision.

But to pursue justice, without seeking wisdom found in facts, logic, and common sense, is moral irresponsibility, when the question concerns something as sacred as life itself. America and Americans can no longer be granted a reprieve from responsibility, averting their eyes and covering their ears to the facts.

The media and some others say that it is poor taste and grisly to publicly show aborted fetuses. I agree. In fact, it is nauseating. Yet look we must, for the issue of abortion involves human babies. All we stand to lose is our lunch; what they stand to lose is their lives.

Today, as nearly one out of three pregnancies ends in abortion,[2] the facts cry out to be examined in the harsh light of reality. As long as there is one shred of doubt in our minds about whether the creature that grows within the wombs of women is a human life or not, we have no moral—or humane—option but to stop. For if it is a tiny, living human being, then stripping it prematurely from its mother's womb and discarding it is taking its life. Thus it is a mistake in morals—a fatal mistake we are making one and a half million times each year.[3]

If anyone can honestly look at what is happening, consider the facts, and still support abortion in good conscience, that is his or her decision—a conscious, informed decision, for which the person who makes it will be held accountable, right or wrong.

At least it will not be a decision made by default, omission, or without due deliberation.

Now let's closely examine the evidence. Consider that the heart of the "fetus" first beats at about twenty-one days[4] and that human brain activity can be recorded at forty-five days of development.[5] The nervous system is developed by twenty days.[6]

One of the founders and primary activists of the National Association for the Repeal of Abortion Laws (NARAL), now the National Abortion Rights League, is Dr. Bernard Nathanson, M.D. After presiding over 60,000 abortions,[7] he has now come full circle and is a pro-life activist. Dr. Nathanson has not only had a change of mind but a change of heart.

In a recent book by Dr. Nathanson, written with Adelle Nathanson, *The Abortion Papers: Inside the Abortion Mentality,* he describes the "heavy baggage of emotion" he still carries. He writes, "The loss of life as a result of my efforts is of such a massive scale that I have no words adequately to express my feelings. They transcend guilt, remorse, regret, contrition, even sorrow and grief."[8]

One American who personally took a close look at the facts is Dr. Jean Staker Garton. An accomplished author, lecturer, and teacher, Dr. Garton was led by her feminist interests to involvement in the area of women's rights and equality, and then into the pro-abortion movement. After examining the evidence, she completely changed her mind about abortion and now actively works in opposition to it. An incident that had profound impact upon Dr. Garton is recounted here in her own words:

> All our children were in bed; the late television news was over, and I was putting the finishing touches to a presentation for medical students scheduled to be given the next day. As I reviewed some slides which might be used, there appeared on the screen a picture of an abortion victim, aged two and one-half months' gestation; her body had been dismembered by a curette, the long-handled knife used in a D&C abortion procedure.
> Suddenly I heard, rather than saw, another person near me. At the sound of a sharp intake of breath, I turned to find that my youngest son, then a sleepy, rumpled three-year-old, had unexpectedly and silently entered the room. His small voice was filled with great sadness as he asked, "Who broke the baby?"

How could this small, innocent child see what so many adults cannot see? How could he know instinctively that this which many people carelessly dismiss as tissue or a blob was one in being with him, was like him? In the words of his question he gave humanity to what adults call "fetal matter"; in the tone of his question he mourned what we exalt as a sign of liberation and freedom. With a wisdom which often escapes the learned, he asked in the presence of the evidence before his eyes, "Who broke the baby?"[9]

That experience was recounted in Dr. Garton's book, *Who Broke the Baby?*

In the same book, Dr. Garton presents some of the insights that led to her growing realization that she could no longer support abortion, but should join in pro-life activities. Dr. Garton writes,

Indoctrination into the language of abortion formed the basis of many of these sessions. "Never accord humanity to what is in the womb," we were told. "Always talk about *the blob,* never the baby." "Stress the woman's rights and her freedom to choose." However, as time passed, I became increasingly uneasy with such arguments, for it seemed to me they involved a semantic deception which, while effective and persuasive, nevertheless lacked integrity. I decided to develop my own argument, one I could debate with honesty, to support a right-to-abort position.

I spent many months of study and research, examining the issue from various disciplines and perspectives. I read the law, medicine and history. I studied Scripture and the church fathers. I worked long and hard to discover evidence to support my theory. But I found none. I had to either face up to reality and change my position or continue to change reality by disguising the truth. It was then, borrowing the words of C. S. Lewis spoken after he converted to the Christian faith he had set out to discredit, that "I was carried kicking and screaming" into the pro-life position "by the sheer weight of the evidence."

The same catchy abortion slogans which I once employed continue to manipulate the feelings and thoughts of many others. The inaccurate ideas fostered by the abortion rhetoric escape the notice of the less critical. Language is an agent for change and when language lies, when words are warped and twisted perversely, they are eventually emptied of their true meaning. The linguistic deception of the pro-abortion argument "tells it like it isn't."[10]

That term *pro-choice* is a good example of what can be done with this type of language manipulation. How can we possibly say that we are opposed to choice? *Choice* is a good word. It implies freedom, and this a land of freedom. Oppose *choice?* How could we? Yet do we support choice, when the choice involves taking the life of another?

When Judeo-Christian principles were the generally accepted and indisputable moral code of our land, we did not as a nation, or as individuals, always live up to them. However, we had a standard against which to measure our actions and an "ideal" toward which to strive. Those principles and that ideal presented us with a vision of what we could become.

Now a moral revolution is being waged in our country, seeking to exchange the Judeo-Christian ethical system of morality for a "no morals" system, or a set of beliefs called "secular humanism."

As this attack on our traditional moral code has been in progress, we can see, if we look with a discerning eye, that the by-products of this grand deception are threatening to destroy the very fiber and the order of our society, bit by bit. Crime on the streets, theft, rape, murder, white-collar crime, drug abuse, drunkenness, spouse abuse, child abuse, governmental graft and many other evils abound today. They are all by-products of immoral living, when measured against Judeo-Christian standards—simply defined as sin. As we seek freedom from those standards, we fall into a bondage of our own creation. In Romans 1:22, Paul says, "Professing themselves to be wise, they became fools" (KJV).

A major aim of the moral revolution is to abolish guilt. Much of the material that advocates loose moral standards identifies guilt as an inhibiting factor. This amounts in practice to abolishing all sense of moral obligation, for we will only feel free from guilt when all sensitivity to moral disapproval is removed. If all moral absolutes are removed and replaced with a "no morals" philosophy, then nothing is considered right or wrong: anything goes. Either there are absolutes or there are *no* absolutes. Logic tells us that if each person chooses his or her own set of absolutes, we will have chaos. We will then have no accepted code of moral conduct to guide our behavior or upon which to base our system of justice. We will have a ship of state without a rudder. There will remain nothing to guide our actions, individually or corporately. And then we will all be victims of those by-products of immorality already listed—and many, many more. I fear many of us are "woefully deceived."

This convoluted reasoning of secular society has extended into the question of abortion. When the secular world has chosen the words and defined the issues, presenting deception by design, society is faced with the gravest danger of all. We may never know about the battle until the war is over.

Dr. Garton cites a very familiar example of a method of self-deception by design:

> . . . Consider how our sophisticated but superstitious society deals with the ill-omened number thirteen. Recall being in a tall building, in an elevator going up, watching the floor numbers as they pass by: 9—10—11—12—14—15. . . . Twelve? Fourteen? What happened to the thirteenth floor? . . . There have been those whose immediate response is, "There isn't any.". . . Of course there is a thirteenth floor. . . . They don't want a thirteenth floor to exist, so they call it something else—the fourteenth floor—in order to avoid the reality of its existence.
>
> Such image distortion is part of an unofficial national game we play, tolerated in general because it is viewed as being quite harmless and sometimes humorous. It is neither harmless nor humorous, however, when that kind of distortion is applied to human beings, for this same thought process (or thought-less process) is plaguing our society as it addresses itself to the life-and-death issue of abortion. The unborn child has become the thirteenth floor of the human family.[11]

Could it be said any better?

How strange it is that women are instinctively endowed with the desire to protect their children, yet abortion rages, wearing the mantle of a righteousness supposedly benefiting those same women. And to compound the paradox, children are the only things in our lives made in the image of God—developed as women work in harmony with His creative hand.

While women are already struggling with their self-esteem,

through abortion society is sending them another negative subliminal message, saying, "The role of being mothers, of bringing
all new life into the world, is not very important. That function,
which is unique unto you, can't be very important, because you
can pluck the fruit of your womb and throw it into the trash
can at will—and it's okay. Therefore, your importance is dimin-
ished."

But that message is not true. Each and every one of us is
important, has value, and the role of motherhood is important.

The joys of motherhood, the fulfillment of a loving home
shared with children being shaped and molded into young adults,
the comforts of grown children and growing grandchildren enjoyed in the autumn and winter years of life—these are conspicu-
ously absent from the public discourse about women's issues,
abortion, and self-fulfillment.

In the January 1984 *Ladies' Home Journal,* Barbara Walters, a
very successful and recognized woman pioneer in the field of
television journalism, acknowledged the historic effect and the
positive changes the women's liberation movement has brought
about. However, she also called woman's greatest accomplishment "the ability to give life and then to nurture that life." In
a moving statement, she went on to express her profound won-
derment at women's God-given ability to have a baby and the
tremendous challenge of carrying on the ages-old role of nurturing a child to healthy adulthood.

Most women today still realize that having children, bearing
new life, is a blessing. But in this same age very contradictory
events are taking place. Some cosmetic firms advertise that their
skin care products contain human placentae, the substance that
nourishes life in the womb. Some claim that the placenta substance used by these firms is primarily obtained from within
the abortion industry. There are "Save the Whale" organizations
and efforts have been made to protect the little fish the snail
darter, but we abort 4,400 human babies a day.[12] Laws exist
to regulate the way animals are killed, requiring they be treated
"humanely" and "rendered insensible to pain." Yet there are
no similar laws to regulate the aborting of human babies.

This is true even though, as we have already noted, at three
weeks after conception the fetus's heart begins to beat, by six

weeks a physician can detect fetal brain activity, and by the eleventh week the fetus has developed sensitivity to touch on the feet and hands and genital areas. There are numerous studies, some in the form of film documentaries, showing that in the second trimester, the twelfth to the twenty-fourth weeks, the fetus responds to electrical stimulation. Many experts believe that the fetus feels pain and is capable of sensation beginning at about two months with the presence of sense receptors and spinal responses.[13]

Legally we maintain the unborn are not human beings. But a U.S. District Court judge in Connecticut has upheld the right of a five-and-a-half-month fetus to sue. A bitter irony indeed.

The following statement from the December 1980 Hastings Center *Report* provides further food for thought:

> Viability . . . the ability to live after birth . . . has been viewed as a milestone endowed with moral and legal significance in the abortion debate. The Supreme Court, in *Roe v. Wade*, found that the pregnant woman's constitutional right of privacy permits her to choose abortion, but only until viability; afterwards, states may restrict her choice in order to save the fetus's life. . . .
>
> If we define viability in light of what the most skillful physicians have been able to do, the time of viability will slip back inexorably toward conception. . . . *Roe v. Wade* could become an anti-abortion decision within a few decades.[14]

Seventeen thousand fetuses were discovered warehoused in formaldehyde-filled containers in California, stored by a clinic collecting fees for ancillary tests allegedly performed upon what some called "pregnancy tissue." Some of that "pregnancy tissue," interestingly enough, formed bodies of babies who had developed up to the seven-and-one-half-month stage of pregnancy. Most of those babies were the children of minority parents. Those minority babies had been denied the most basic of their civil rights, the right to life itself.

The seventeen thousand are not buried yet, more than two years after they were discovered. This is because of a restraining order filed by the American Civil Liberties Union and the Feminist Women's Health Center (and abortion clinic) on June 8, 1982, denying burial.[15] Burial, you see, implies life was present before they were aborted and their development terminated.

The January 20, 1977, *Sacramento Bee* reports sewers were found clogged by the arms and legs of what some are wont to call "pregnancy tissue." In areas where abortion is a thriving business, disposability of the waste in the industry is a problem.

The abortion business is, incidentally, a *big business,* having an estimated income of $700 million a year.[16] Greed dictates that it will not die easily nor without great resistance.

In the classified section of the December 22, 1983, *Des Moines Register,* the following ad appeared in the personals column: "ABORTIONS BY CERT. GYN. REAS." Above that advertisement was: "FIX YOUR VACUUM RIGHT OR NO CHARGE. BARGAINS." Below the abortion ad was: "Santa Suits for Rent $10 and up. Reserve now." A poignant commentary. Explanation not required.

A shocking manifestation of the abortion industry has recently become a matter of concern in this country—the possible use of abortion by-products in the beauty industry, specifically, collagen-based cosmetics. Collagen is the gelatinous substance found in the connective tissue, cartilage, and bone of animals and humans. The use of human placentae and human collagens obtained through abortion is being written about and researched increasingly by those opposed to abortion and distressed by the magnitude of its occurrences. It has long been alleged that the use of aborted humans is a frequent practice in parts of Europe. Some in the pro-life community are convinced that the practice has spread to this country. If this were proven to be true, I believe that many purchasers of beauty products containing collagen would be greatly disturbed and become very cautious when selecting cosmetics containing collagen, using only those products clearly identified as utilizing animal or synthetic collagens. To allow an additional profit line to the human abortion industry would be very difficult to justify with a clear conscience, it would seem.

Brenda, the former activist in the feminist movement whom I mentioned earlier, explained how she dealt with the issue before coming to Christ. When discussing abortion, she said, "That was always a hard issue for me, because I knew it was wrong. However, I wanted to rationalize why it was all right. When I took a bio-medical ethics course in college, I had to take a position on abortion and defend it morally. Though I took the pro-abortion stand in that paper, I discovered I could never defend it morally. That discovery contradicted where I was coming from in my head and I really struggled. I did come to the conclusion that there was *no* way to defend abortion morally. I think most feminists know that. But there are a lot of practical reasons feminists can come up with to defend abortion. For example, they talk about economics and fairness. Many times the father has abandoned the mother and the baby, perhaps leaving her without a source of support. That really doesn't justify the fact that the mother abandons the baby in the ultimate way."

Some feminists are extremely adamant about their stand on abortion. In the September 1, 1983, issue of *USA Today*, Gloria Steinem, co-founder of *Ms.* magazine and a leader in the feminist movement, was asked, "What does feminism hope to accomplish in the next decade?"

Ms. Steinem responded, "We want to establish reproductive freedom as a basic right—a fifth freedom—as important as freedom of speech, or freedom of assembly, so that women cannot be told by the government or anyone else to have or not to have children, but can, at least, control our own bodies. And we want to be an equal part of the Constitution."

An ironic coincidence, is it not, that the push for reproductive freedom, allowing abortion on demand, comes at the same point in history when there are available the most convenient, effective, and greatest variety of birth control methods? Though the religious beliefs of some do not allow for the use of contraceptives, the term coined by pro-choicers, *mandatory pregnancy*, is a misnomer.

If a woman does not want a baby, she has no need for an abortion—if she makes the *correct choices* at the appropriate time, and has had *control of her own body* in the appropriate manner. Like it or not, life requires responsibility for our actions. Can we, in good conscience, shift the responsibility for poor choices and lack of control of our bodies to the innocent unborn, who have never had a choice? Should a helpless and defenseless child suffer the consequences of our actions at the sacrifice of its life? Have we so numbed our consciences?

The views of two world-recognized women should give us all a reason to pause to reflect. Mother Teresa of Calcutta said,

"As for countries that have enacted laws permitting abortions as a so-called natural act, we must pray for them, because the sin is great. . . . For the rest of their lives they would never forget that as mothers they had killed their children."[17] And the late Golda Meir, prime minister of Israel, a woman universally recognized for outstanding world leadership, perhaps second to none, said without hesitation that to have a baby was the most fulfilling thing a woman could ever do.[18]

A growing number of alternatives are being provided for those who might otherwise seek an abortion. Springing up across the country are many homes for unwed mothers, adoption services, and even groups providing assistance to unwed mothers who decide to keep their babies. One example of the latter is a facility called Mom's House in Johnstown, Pennsylvania. The children are cared for during the day while their mothers complete their schooling. The mothers are given tutoring and provided with transportation. This project is staffed and financed by various individuals and groups in the local community.

The tide of opposition to abortion is growing in this country, as more people become educated to the facts and stop to consider what is really happening when a baby is aborted.

This is what happens in some of the most common methods of abortion:

In suction curettage, the most popular method, a suction machine is used to draw the baby out of the mother's womb.

In dilation and curettage (D&C), the physician uses a curette, a long-handled surgical knife, and reaches up into the womb and cuts, dislodges, and removes the baby. In this method, the baby is dismembered and great care must be taken to assure that all the parts are extracted, since they could cause infection within the mother.

A third method involves injecting a saline (salty) solution into the womb through the mother's abdominal wall. Caution must be taken, because the mother could suffer painful burning if any of the solution were to get into her tissue. The saline solution burns and poisons the baby, and it is born through labor within twenty-four hours. Usually it is dead; if not, it generally dies shortly thereafter, if left unattended. Some have been known to live, if cared for.

Abortions in late term are sometimes surgically removed by

a method exactly like delivery by Caesarean section and set aside to die.[19]

Since the Supreme Court *Roe v. Wade* decision in 1973, creating the possibility of legalized abortions through the ninth month, fifteen million babies have been aborted in the United States.[20] In June 1983, in consideration of an abortion question, Justice Sandra Day O'Connor wrote a dissenting minority opinion in which Justices White and Rehnquist joined.

In the dissent Justice O'Connor wrote, ". . . *Potential* life is no less potential in the first weeks of pregnancy than it is at viability or afterward. At any stage in pregnancy, there is the *potential* for human life."

O'Connor also noted, ". . . State action 'encouraging childbirth except in the most urgent circumstances' is 'rationally related to the legitimate government objective of protecting potential life.' "[21]

There are grave moral problems and problems of logic incurred as fetology, the medical treatment of the fetus in the womb as a patient, becomes more advanced, and modern medicine saves premature babies born at increasingly earlier ages.[22]

Recent evidence of the ethical dilemma of physicians is noted in the *New York Times* of February 15, 1984. The headline on the two-page story is "When Abortion Becomes Birth: A Dilemma of Medical Ethics Shaken by New Advances." The article begins with the story of a baby which was aborted, yet lived. It goes on to say,

> In effect, medical technology has leaped beyond both the law on abortion and the assumptions of medical ethics. At many hospitals, policies have been thrown into turmoil.
>
> Doctors are grappling with whether a child born as a result of an abortion should be given the same extraordinary care as one born of a miscarriage. Hospital ethics committees are confronting the question of whether late abortions should be moved out of operating rooms and into obstetrical wings holding the latest life-saving equipment. Women requesting late abortions at some hospitals are being told that a fetus born alive will be given all chances to survive. . . .
>
> Because infants born of abortion are injured in the abortion process, legal scholars are asking whether it would be possible for such a seriously injured infant to make a claim of "wrongful life" against a hospital.[23]

Physicians' perceptions may be changing in light of dynamic advances in fetal diagnosis and care which clearly distinguish a fetus from its mother for treatment purposes.[24]

January 21, 1984, commemorating the eleventh anniversary of the *Roe v. Wade* Supreme Court decision, seventy thousand people from across the country came to Washington, D.C., to participate in a March for Life. It was an enormous gathering although the event received no greater press coverage than had been given at times when fifty or sixty pro-choice advocates had demonstrated in the past. The 1984 rally attested the fact that pro-life support is increasing.

In 1973 there were some who predicted that the legalization of abortion would open a moral "Pandora's box" which would lead to infanticide, the killing of children after birth, and euthanasia. Most felt that such early voices came from irrational alarmists. Yet eleven years later we find that infanticide is no longer a rare occurrence. There have even been court cases where infanticide has been defended as proper, as well as lawful. We read and hear about more and more cases around the country where handicapped infants are pushed into the corner of hospital nurseries and denied food and water, as well as medical care. This has occurred when some person, or group of people, decided that, in their opinion, these infants would not have a "quality life." Some have dubbed our society's declining respect for life and loss of moral standards as "domino decadence," one thing leading to another. We also find euthanasia and suicide being discussed in a changing moral and philosophical light today. We seem to have developed the "ethic of human disposability." Human life has come to be considered expendable, when deemed appropriate by some.

The issue is no longer one just of abortion, but rather of the "sanctity of human life." The question is, *is human life sacred anymore?* It appears that mankind has started "playing God." But we shouldn't attempt to "play God" unless we're qualified. I have never met anyone who was, and I doubt that anyone else has.

The July 1983 issue of *Pediatrics,* the professional journal of the American Academy of Pediatrics, carried an article by Dr. Peter Singer, an Australian pediatrician, in which he urged that we replace concern for the "sanctity of human life" with concern for the "quality of human life." Dr. Singer wrote,

If we compare a severely defective human infant with a nonhuman animal, a dog or a pig, for example, we will often find the nonhuman to have superior capacities, both actual and potential, for rationality, self-consciousness, communication, and anything else that can plausibly be considered morally significant. Only the fact that the defective infant is a member of the species *Homo sapiens* leads it to be treated differently from the dog or pig. Species membership alone, however, is not morally relevant.[25]

When we have lost respect for human life, it has great impact on all human relationships. Changes of attitude, subtle though they be, creep into society, as seen in the above article.

In a column in the *Washington Post* of October 20, 1983, Courtland Milloy wrote, "There is a high infant mortality here, a high rate of teen-age pregnancy and abortion and now a 25 percent increase in child abuse and sexual assault on children over the same period last year."

If life before birth, even a few weeks before birth, can be taken and is not sacred, why should it be any different immediately after birth—or several months, or years later? If a child's life can morally, and even legally, be taken when it is inconvenient or not performing according to our standards at *one* time, why wouldn't the same rules apply at most *any* time?

If some one, or group of people, can make decisions about who is capable of living a "quality life" immediately after birth, how long will it be before decisions like these are made about the maimed, the infirm, the handicapped, the elderly? How long would it be until their fatal judgments might fall upon you or me, or someone we love?

Another seldom-voiced issue involved in the abortion question is concern for the "second victim" of abortion, the mother. Several organizations have recently formed to uphold the cause of women in what they see as an exploitive industry. WEBA (Women Exploited by Abortion) was founded in September of 1983. A short eight months after its genesis, it had grown from two people to twenty thousand members in forty-five states with one hundred thirty-five chapters.

Nancyjo Mann, the founder of WEBA and a woman who has personally suffered extensively from undergoing an abortion, says:

. . . My case is not unusual at all. People want to say, "Oh, but Nancy, you're the extreme." That's not true. In fact there are so many more of us than there are the other. The emotional hurt is so deep. You do not discuss your abortion, the suction machines and the needles and everything else, over a cup of tea and a cookie. Women just don't do this. The pain is just too deep and too great.

I'm sure there are women out there who are never fazed, never, by their abortion. But I would say that 98, 99 percent of them *are* fazed, whether it's for a small period of time or for the rest of their life, whether they suffer only a small degree or die from their abortions.[26]

Nancyjo went on to describe some of the painful after-effects of abortion for many and has presented her story in testimony before a Congressional Committee. She is very grateful that she has found healing in the forgiveness and love of Christ, whom she came to know some years after her traumatic abortion.

There will always be an "empty crib" in the hearts of women who have aborted their babies. But they too can find forgiveness in Christ who has unconditional love for them and stands ever ready to forgive.

God's Word shows us that abortion is wrong, a sin. It always has been, and God's laws are not subject to change or amendment. The Bible tells us that Christ was but a few months developed in the womb of His mother, Mary, when John the Baptist, in the womb of his mother, Elizabeth, leaped with joy to be in His presence (Luke 1:41). Jeremiah 1:5 records that God told Jeremiah that He knew him before he was formed in the womb. And Psalm 139:15–16 tells that God knew us before we were born and while we were in our mothers' wombs.

Had that little girl named Mary, some two thousand years ago, done what today's society would have encouraged—for she had all the reasons—Jesus Christ could have been "the thirteenth floor." But she was willing to be known, very simply, as "somebody's mother." She considered it a blessing.

Positions and Priorities

The Lord gives the command;
The women who proclaim the good tidings
    are a great host.

Psalm 68:11 NASB

An old, old, humble woman, faithfully seeking God in prayer day and night in the place of worship, beheld the infant Christ child. And thanking God, Anna began telling everyone in Jerusalem, "The Messiah has come" (Luke 2:36–38).

After that child had become a man, a simple and unlikely Samaritan woman, on a dusty, hot day, brought the entire community to seek and discover the Messiah, who had told her who He was. They came because "she went and told" (John 4:28–29).

Another woman, weeping because His body was gone from the tomb, turned and was the first to see the risen Lord. He spoke her name, "Mary." Recognizing Him, she said, "Rabboni," (teacher), and she ran and told the disciples that Jesus had come back to life (John 20:11–18).

These women, all living in New Testament times, had their priorities straight. It had not always been that way for all of them, but Jesus made the difference. He brought them to wholeness and fulfillment, and He chose them to fill profoundly significant roles. Each in her own special, unique way, played a vital part in His ministry as He walked this earth.

The Bible says that the Lord is the same, yesterday, today, and forever. And women who allow Him to order their priorities can be just as significant today as in that earlier era.

We have an even greater challenge today, for we can no longer see Him with our eyes. But Jesus said, ". . . Blessed are they that have not seen, and yet have believed" (John 20:29). Addi-

tionally, we live in a day when secular society scoffs at a belief
in the things of God, which are beyond the material and cannot
be arrived at by human scientific formulas. While that makes
the challenge greater, it also makes the opportunity greater, for
there is a deep need, a deep hunger in the hearts of people
today. Today's world needs to hear the Good News that Jesus
brings. We need a Savior.

This is a time in human history when women in this country
can have a culture-changing, yes, even a world-changing influence. Since we live in the United States, we help shape her
face to the rest of the world. Even though there are some who
criticize the position of women in this country today, we are
still fortunate to have the most and the best of everything, measured against the other countries of the world. Culturally, because of our opportunities, we can have great influence here at
home. Because America is the leader of the free world, we are
observed by other nations, and our attitudes and actions affect
the world. The shape of our culture affects other cultures in
other lands in a variety of ways. In the wise words of Rosalie
Mills Appleby, "Christ is the only transforming power there is
and we strive in vain without Him, whether we are building a
life or a country."[1]

As society has advanced in industry and commerce, technology
and science, education and knowledge, we have been able to
change our standard of living, but not necessarily improve our
lives. We have expanded our capabilities, but often have not
improved our attitudes. We have improved our overall health,
but we are unable to heal lonely, hurting hearts.

The increasing despair, fear, depression, broken relationships
and broken homes, crime and corruption, strife and violence
among nations—the ongoing struggles of mankind—speak
loudly of our need beyond ourselves. As late twentieth century
mankind, a powerful giant, advances rapidly in the advent of
the twenty-first century, the exterior strength of its hulk and
the sophistications of its rhetoric are impugned by its interior
weakness.

An unknown author expressed it well. "The very helplessness
of the world today is in itself a repudiation of that self-sufficient
view of life that the world in its progressive development has
outgrown the need for Christ. It is following Christ that gives

the world what it most needs—a standard of right living, a cause to maintain and defend, a Leader to follow, and a law to obey."[2]

The timeless has been sacrificed for the timely. The eternal has been replaced with the temporal. Present-day humankind is in need of the sensitive, nurturing, virtuous influence of women, women of God. There is a need for life-changing experiences that will enable each of us, as we go into our slice of the world, to take to our brothers and sisters the love and compassion that can correct the course of society.

Wilhelmina, the former Queen of the Netherlands, said, "Christ led me to the experience of overwhelming reality. . . . What this means in a life of unknown liberation, perspective, joy and general change cannot be told in words."[3]

Jesus is the one person we can totally trust to always love us, to always be with us, to always appreciate us, and to never fail us in any way. No human being can live up to those standards.

In *Her Name Is Woman,* author Gien Karssen tells stories of some of the outstanding women of biblical history. One is the story about Mary, the woman who sat at the feet of the Lord to learn, over the objections of her sister, Martha. Speaking about the time when Jesus and His disciples had first come to Mary's home, Karssen says:

He [Jesus] had also entered her [Mary's] life and—as He alone could do—had brought about a radical change. She didn't recognize her own life anymore. "He started by giving us His friendship," she mused. That was an unknown experience. Up until that time a wide gulf had existed between men and women. After all, didn't the Jewish men thank God every morning in their prayers that He has created them "not as slave, nor a heathen nor a woman"?

It had been apparent immediately that He was different. His concern was not just for a woman. He was interested in the total human being, man or woman.

He had introduced a new respect for women. He had offered her possibilities that had been unknown until then. He had lifted her to His plan. That was why she had felt so entirely at ease in his presence. Without any shyness, she had come and sat down in the midst of the men who were listening to His words.

Sitting at His feet and listening to Him, there was a hunger in her heart, a thirst after God. The purpose of her existence had become clear in listening to this man. A conviction grew within her, "I am created for God. I exist because of Him."[4]

The story Karssen relates took place when Jesus and His disciples were at the home of Martha, Mary, and Lazarus shortly before the Passover, when Jesus would go to His death (John 12:1–8). Mary took some extremely costly perfume, which was used as an embalming oil, and broke the bottle and poured it on the feet of Jesus, wiping them with her hair, as an expression of her gratitude.

Judas Iscariot, who not many days later would betray Jesus, objected and criticized Mary, saying that the money it cost should have been given to the poor. But Jesus spoke in her defense, knowing the sincere intent of her heart. Karssen writes:

> Quietly listening to His words had helped Mary grow into a woman with spiritual insight. She had become a woman who understood the secrets of God. She knew precisely what to do and when.
>
> The Master's words not only revealed Mary's thoughts—they also clarified the way God looked at things. His highest praise was reserved for the person who was interested in His Word and who acted upon it. Such a person didn't need to fear criticism from his fellow men. He didn't need to withdraw when they nagged at him. Such a person had the best advocate available— Jesus Himself.
>
> Again Mary was not rebuked. On the contrary, right then Jesus erected a monument for her that would stand through the ages. It was better than any monument of stone or bronze. "Now remember this! Wherever the Gospel is preached, what she has done will be told about her."
>
> The smell of Mary's perfume has permeated the entire world— even to this day. Thousands, no, millions have praised her. They have been stimulated by her, because she did what she could. Mary was a woman with insight who chose the best.[5]

When the call to choose the best *has been answered* by women, then we ask pastors to teach us, equip us for ministry—to live in the world and not be conformed to it. Rather, as we are transformed by Christ, we will be able to work at transforming the world around us.

I would ask pastors then to allow women to use their gifts. I suggest that pastors ask themselves, have they entrusted to women within the Church roles as important as the ones that Jesus gave to them? As we walk through the Scriptures, we can look for the times when God entrusted to women vitally important roles, for He knew they were loyal, faithful servants at heart—compassionate and wise. He never doubted or overlooked their abilities. Have we?

I recognize that the issue of women's positions within the organized church is a subject of debate. There are several points of view and many Christians today are rethinking their past views in light of God's leading. They have become more open to examining the Scriptures in a broader context, not accepting a doctrinal view based upon one or two isolated verses.

While some do not believe that women should be involved in any type of ministry, some believe women can pastor churches. Yet others believe women can minister, but only under the spiritual authority of a man.

A statement by Max Call based on Genesis 2:20–24 in his article "Understanding God's Wisdom" in the August 1982 *Christ for the Nations Newsletter*, represents an impartial point of view: "God in His perfection is plural. He is everything. He contains both male and female. When He created Adam in His image, Adam contained both male and female. Then God took the female out of man and made woman. When He did this He made man and woman equally incomplete in His image."

Dr. Paul Yonggi Cho, pastor of the largest church in the world, in Seoul, Korea, with 250,000 members, says women are an important and extensive part of the ministry in his home cell groups. Their role is modeled after that of the women in Paul's ministry, who served in many significant ways, but always under Paul's spiritual authority.

Further views are expressed in the following statements by a variety of today's Christian leaders:

> "The need to nurture is much stronger in most women than it is in men. . . . More women should be involved in professional counseling. A professional counselor who is a woman has an intuitive side that really contributes to the professional side" (Ruth Senter, contributing editor for *Today's Christian Woman*).

"Women have been given spiritual gifts in the church just as men have, but these gifts are to be used within God's framework of order. . . . Very often, though, women's frustrations rise out of their unwillingness to take the place of servitude. Until we are willing to do that which is least, God can't make us ruler over many things" (Elisabeth Elliot, well-known author, lecturer, and retreat leader).

"We need to create structures outside the formal worship—when the church gathers to sing, to pray, to be joyful, for example— where both men and women can use their gifts" (Bruce Waltke, Old Testament scholar and professor, Regent College, Vancouver, B.C.).

"God has equipped women for a variety of ministries—in the home, the church, the community. He gives spiritual gifts to both men and women—they ought to be utilized" (Howard Hendricks, author and professor, Dallas Theological Seminary).

"There are two freedoms in the Charismatic circles which don't exist otherwise. These have encouraged women to become freer in their expression. . . . These freedoms have given a new release to women who for years in their classic churches were either inadvertently or directly taught to be silent. . . . With the freedom of expression has come the freedom to be leaders" (Iverna Tompkins, author, teacher, and former pastor).[6]

One closing thought that perhaps says it all is by Dr. Richard Lovelace, professor of church history at Gordon-Conwell Theological Seminary, South Hamilton, Massachusetts:

And the male who always assumes an authoritarian role toward women, and never honors their gifts and intelligence by listening for the correcting voice of the Spirit speaking through them, is also risking disobedience and weakened fellowship with God. If we are always seeking to "serve one another through love" the question of "who's boss?" will fade into the background as both sexes submit themselves to the lordship of Christ.[7]

The debate goes on. But the most important question is not what is our position, but rather, are our own personal priorities in order? Do we, men and women, want to serve the Lord more than we want anything for ourselves? Is seeking His will for our lives our first priority? Being involved in any form of ministry position is not like choosing a profession to enter. It must be a calling or we will be operating under our own power, and that is never going to be enough.

In her book *The Worth of a Woman,* Iverna Tompkins says, "God is restoring His church. He has given a hungering, thirsting spirit to many. People won't respond to lectures; we need to minister in the Spirit. By getting a theological degree, don't think you have the right to minister. . . . God's anointing will make a place for you. If God has placed His hand on you for full-time ministry, you won't be able to do anything but that."[8]

Heeding God's "call" for His purposes in our lives is valid for us all, men and women.

Sadly, for some today, preaching seems to have become just a polished art form, designed to hold an audience, identical to the approach of secular public speaking. If God's Spirit isn't in it, our efforts will be limited to the human level alone and the power of God will not flow. I heard a pastor say recently: "The Church has to turn to a deep love of Christ, seeking to please God. We need to know God and listen to Him, to see what He wants—not give Him what religion says He wants. We have come to worship 'worship.' When the Church loves the Church, it is a perversion—like a man loving a man, or a woman loving a woman. The Church must love Christ."

In the December 18, 1983, *Washington Post,* a young black nun was quoted in a section entitled "Women Religious." When she was asked, "Why would a young woman today want to be a nun?" she responded beautifully: "People ask me that all the time. . . . By having nothing, I am free to give everything. I can go where there is need, and serve God by serving his people. Which brings me greatest joy. . . . With the Lord's help I wanted to be a witness for him here on Earth." How different her attitude is from that of another nun quoted in a separate article. That nun described herself as "mad as hell" about the positions of women within her Church.

To the Lord, the attitude of our hearts is key. Are our priorities in order?

If we—men and women—demand from human beings recognition for ourselves, the most we can receive is what humans can give to us. If we seek God and His righteousness first, we will receive from Him things that humans do not possess to give, and much more. As we empty ourselves of the "big me," we are filled full of those treasures that money can't buy and human beings can't produce.

So many women today are hurting and insecure inside and are misled by a culture that demands position and title to signify importance. "Rebellion" wears many faces, so we must guard our motives, for our hearts are deceitful. We kid ourselves about our nature, but God knows our true motives. In Luke 16:15, Jesus said, "You are those who justify yourselves before men, but God knows your hearts . . ." (rsv). He is concerned about our attitudes, and if he wants us to have position, he will lead us there.

At the risk of sounding stuck on the same note, I mention Mother Teresa's life again, because I think it contains so many wonderful examples for us. It portrays a powerful principle from the hand of God. This meek little woman, who has sought no position, who has no worldly goods, and who is uncomfortable in the limelight, has been raised by God to a pinnacle of recognition. I'm told that this recipient of the Nobel Prize, when asked what she does, often responds that she is good at cleaning toilets. God truly has used "the simple to confound the wise."

God's order is established for good reasons. The inherent strengths that men and women have been given by their Creator, when used properly, fit together in a harmonious completeness. However, our greatest strengths can become our greatest weaknesses when overstressed. The deep spiritual sensitivity of women allows them to have hearing hearts open to the still small voice of God. But it also, in the extreme, makes them more susceptible to spiritual deception. Men, on the other hand, are likely to be more susceptible to struggles with ego and the misuse of authority.

In recent days there are more and more women who are entering into some form of ministry within the Church. I think of some of the wives I have come to know who are now co-pastoring with their husbands: John and Anne Gimenez at Rock Church in Virginia Beach, Virginia; Bob and Marti Tilton, who have built the Word of Faith satellite ministry out of Dallas, Texas, and Charles and Rochelle Nieman, who have the largest church in El Paso, Texas. The list is long and these are but a few.

Various national Christian television ministries involve both the husbands and wives, and the ministry of wives with their husbands in various evangelical ministries is also widespread. For example, two dear friends of ours, Bill and Vonette Bright, are the founders of Campus Crusade for Christ. Vonette has labored as a teammate with Bill for many years, her role changing as the seasons of their lives have changed.

Many women have powerful, distinctly individual ministries—in Scripture teaching, speaking, writing, and other areas. Certainly not to be overlooked are the wives of pastors across the land who have a powerful influence and make a tremendous contribution to church ministries. The positive impact of these women is too great to be measured.

Though opinions vary on the issue of women in ministry, if you were to ask these and other women about their ministries, I think that most of them would tell you they have placed themselves in the church under the spiritual authority of their husbands, who are also pastors, or they are under men who are in spiritual authority within the Church. I think you would also find that they would also tell you that God has raised them up to their present positions with the approval and encouragement of their husbands. They have not had to push and shove to attain that position.

We may rejoice in what God is doing through these women, not wasting our energy and emotion trying to judge if they are doing too much or not enough. Only the Lord can make those judgments.

Now I have a heart-cry for the pastors of this country, and I pray that they will hear this message. For, from where will the call to Christ sound forth, if not from God's people, His Church?

The Bible admonishes us that there must be unity in the Body of believers in order for the powerful works of God to be accomplished. And God's people need to be heard loud and clear in today's world, heard speaking forth not in condemnation but in conviction. Not in self-righteousness, but in His righteousness. Not in anger and denunciation, but in love. (But not the brand of love that is oversentimentalized acceptance and understanding of any and all behavior and beliefs, which could be termed "sloppy *agapē.*")

Instead, God's church needs to speak the truth, in love. As

Jesus did, we are to hate the sin and love the sinner. The catch is, it is impossible to do that without His presence within us pouring out *His* love, a totally unconditional, true *agapē* love.

Unfortunately, cloaking worldly ideas and attitudes in spiritual garb and godly talk, some today have taken the world into the Church rather than taken Christ into the world. We don't need to have our ears tickled from the pulpits today, merely hearing what is comfortable. There are times when ministers need to make our ears burn—with truth. Christ called us to be salt— to salt the world with God's truth. Salt stings, and people are inclined to return in kind. The truth sometimes hurts and people react harshly. But this is a world hungry for truth, and hungry for people strong enough, confident enough, and committed enough to speak it.

Many of America's women are hungry and hurting on the inside, and they need to hear that Jesus is real, that He loves them, values them, and wants to use them. He has designed them to perform a task that men cannot duplicate, try as they will. Women are the heart of mankind.

Intelligent and wise, yet gentle-spirited, sensitive, and compassionate, women can communicate love in a way that is special and God-designed. They need to be told from the pulpits how important they are and they need to be appreciated. If the pulpits of this country will sound forth the call of Christ to women, the women He loves, the response will be overwhelming. We have a country full of women who need to know that God loves and values them, and we have a country full of men who need to be reminded how really vital women are to all of society. If it were not for women, neither men nor society would be where they are today. Many need to have their attitudes reshaped by the Author of Justice, Christ.

What men and women hear from the world today about women's identity and worth are demands and resistance—charges and countercharges. Why should the world, by default of the church, have to be the champion of fairness and justice for women? There will be no need, if the church of Christ will stand in the gap—will take His love into the homes and into the marketplace of the country. For if the world presents an answer to what is really a moral problem, that answer will be filtered through its current set of social mores, not provided in light of the truth of the ages.

When women, or men, do not understand the value, dignity, and worth they have in Christ, they try to find it elsewhere. If women buy into the cultural mindset, which some in the feminist movement present, that our jobs will make us more important, it will only be a temporary cover-up for their insecurities.

This is a plea to the ministers in this country to call women to become all that God created us to be. Don't let us complacently live beneath our spiritual heritage. Don't let us buy into the world's system, for it will leave us empty and still hurting after we've tried it. Don't let us, or the world, intimidate you. Make us shape up, women and men. Don't let us accept the world's distortion of who we are. Remind us women we are not second-class citizens in God's economy. We are *all* equal in worth before God. Remind us all that we have *no* rights of our own that are not gifts to us from God. They are free gifts, to be accepted with *appreciation*. We should then honor the rights of others, recognizing them as *their* gifts from a loving Father. Remind us if we got what we deserved, we'd all be in trouble. Remind us of our need for salvation. Tell us of God's mercy—point us to Christ.

Remind us that what the world considers important will all pass away and that our lives are short and quickly gone. We need to hear it. The voices of the world are breaking our eardrums and *we can't hear you*. Don't tell us about one denomination's doctrine being right and another's being wrong. Tell us about Christ, the only One who has perfect doctrine and total revelation. Tell us, in Christ we can love our enemies. Tell us to stand up for His righteousness without fear of ridicule and scorn. Tell us we can be leaders in our own individual lives.

We know some of you are well-intentioned and have the best interests of women at heart, but don't try to appease us or give us recognition by working to change pronouns and terms in order to desex the language of the Bible. That appears as though you think the "blue smoke and mirrors" of a language change could bring identity and fulfillment. What we need is a change of *heart*, not a change of *words*.

Instead, call to America's women and introduce us to the true Liberator, Jesus Christ! Affirm us in our full womanhood, which we will only find in Him, His love, and His plan for our lives.

The Call to Excellence

To me, success is doing what God wants
you to do and doing it with a commitment
to excellence. I feel that I'm doing what God
wants me to be doing. I must do it well.
If I do it well, then the effects of it will
be multiplied and the rewards will come—
I don't have to worry about that. . . .
Success is a moving target. . . . . Success
moves as we grow in life.
Whatever the job is, do it the very best you
can, and make it shine.

Mary Crowley

The neighbors just marveled at her. Why, you would think that she'd have to be a human dynamo to do all the things she did! Yet she never was out of sorts and never complained.

Complaining—that, it seemed, was what some of her neighbor women spent most of their time doing. If they weren't grumbling about their husbands for not paying enough attention to them or appreciating them enough, it was about something else. You'd think that nothing ever went right for them. They seemed to see themselves as the victims of somebody or something all the time. Victims of "life," maybe.

Yet here was "Mrs. Perfection," seeming to do everything so much better than they did. The lights in her house were on early in the morning. She actually enjoyed getting a big breakfast ready for the kids and her husband, Phil, before they left the house. She said she planned the rest of her day in the morning, too. Can you imagine anyone so organized?

The women would talk about her sometimes when they got together for lunch. Still, they just couldn't criticize her, for she seemed to love everyone. She was so kind and friendly. She'd give you anything she had, if you needed it. Not only did she make clothes for her family, she would also sew for the needy in town. And speaking of sewing, the gowns she made for herself looked like designer creations. She was amazing!

Some might feel envious of all she could do, but they just couldn't help liking her. In fact, she was the one they all turned to for advice when they were having troubles in their lives.

Yes, they did all love her, but she made them uncomfortable with themselves.

The women were talking about her one morning as they gathered outside the market. She had just gone by, calling out a "hello" as she passed.

"Did you hear about the great deal she made on that land last week?" Rebecca asked. "She bought it last month and sold it Thursday at a big profit. Where does she get that good business sense? Maybe she's just lucky."

Donna disagreed, "No, I think she just has a knack for business. We all know how well she manages their employees. Why, Phil is always bragging about her down at the city council. 'My wife did this and my wife did that.' My husband said Phil told him that now she's developed a little business selling some of those fancy clothes she makes. I'll tell you, she's been a big help to Phil."

Linda interjected, "I went by their house yesterday and she was out there working with the hired help in the field. Doesn't she ever get sick of all that work? It will make an old lady out of her before her time."

"Oh, come on, Linda," Rebecca responded. "You know she looks better than anybody I know. She keeps herself up, and getting old doesn't even bother her. I mentioned getting old the other day and she said she actually looks forward to it."

Donna summed it all up as she said, "Well, when it comes right down to it, you know we are all just jealous. She's really a great gal. How many mothers do you know these days whose teen-age kids go around telling how great they think their mother is?"

"Yes," Linda said, "you're right. Phil and the kids are lucky to have someone like her. But then, they know it." Pensive, she added, "Do you suppose her approach to life has anything to do with her faith? I know she spends a lot of time reading the Bible and praying. When my mother died last year, she was more comfort to me than my pastor was. I think that's her secret—her faith."

And who, you may wonder, is this special woman of the '80s, who has it all together? In truth, she is not a modern-day product of "women's lib." No, she is the "Proverbs 31 woman." In the last chapter in the Book of Proverbs, the question is posed, "A worthy woman who can find?" And the response follows, "For her price is far above rubies" (31:10). There is no doubt about it, the Old Testament account of the attributes of an ideal worthy woman describes a woman who is no slouch.

There are some today who believe that to be a Christian woman means that you are extremely limited in what you can do. They stereotype the Christian woman as a drab, dull person who seldom ventures forth from her home. This idea is completely false, far removed from what a Christian woman can quite properly be. It is time to discard the old stereotypes and look at what the Lord has really called us to be.

In point of fact, we are called not only to use our talents, but the Lord calls us to excellence in all that we do. In Ephesians 6:6–7 we are told that, no matter what our position in life, we are to "do all things as unto the Lord," as though we were doing them for *Him*—which calls for nothing but our very best.

In Matthew 25:14–30, Jesus tells a parable revealing that He not only calls upon us to use our talents, but even more, we will be held accountable for what we do with them. In the parable, the master called his servants to him. He gave one servant five talents (units of money). To the second he gave two talents, and to the third he gave one talent. The first and the second servants went out right away and invested—used—the talents they were given, doubling them. The third, not wanting to take a chance, buried his.

When their master returned, the first and second servants gave him the talents he had given them plus the additional amount from the investment of them. He commended them, saying that they would be entrusted with even more now because of their proper use of the talents. But the servant who buried his received a very strong rebuke and was told that the talent that had been entrusted to him would be taken away and given to the servant with the ten talents.

Jesus was telling his followers through this simple story that we should use our talents. We are accountable for them, and if we use them well, He will entrust more to us. This is a strong message to us all, in any and all of the life roles we may play throughout the seasons of our lives. Most of us have undiscovered or undeveloped talents, capabilities that are untapped. When we utilize what has been entrusted to us, we find that a sense of fulfillment and blessing follows. It feels good to exercise our gifts; it brings a sense of accomplishment.

If you are a mother working at home, there is no need for the time spent there to be boring or personally unproductive. In fact, there are some wonderful aspects of being the master of your own time and schedule. True, you have to schedule your time around the needs of others, but then, don't you generally have to do this in a job or position outside the home also? You schedule your time to meet the needs of your clients, your patients, your boss, your customers—or whomever. In the marketplace or in the home, you still have to fit into the needs or requirements of others. There is no great release and independence of time when you are employed in the work force. That is a fact of life.

It seems that some women are afraid of being in charge of their own time at home. A structured work situation does provide a sense of security. But at home you have the opportunity and challenge of mastering your own time to the best advantage to yourself and others.

At home you are still responsible to develop your talents, and that can be done in many ways. Be creative. You could take some courses in which you are interested. You could start a local or neighborhood project to meet community needs or to help the needy. You could study child development and determine to raise your children to the best of your ability.

Set goals and meet them, for we all need challenges. Get organized. Manage your home as you would a small business, while still developing a warm, loving environment with a happy spirit in the home. Establish family traditions—traditions which make memories to be cherished and recalled by your children into their adult years, then passed on to their children.

Keep yourself current on national and world news and happenings. You will then be more interested and interesting to your family and friends. Keep up on your husband's work activities and involve him in your interests and work. This mutual sharing contributes to a healthy relationship.

Very frankly, I feel that women who work in the home and never have anything to talk about except household activities can be boring. When I was at home with young children, I remember that there was a woman with whom I dreaded to get stuck for an entire evening. It seemed all she talked about were dirty diapers and trivia. I loved being a mother and enjoyed discussing our children, but I wanted and needed some additional mental stimulation. A woman who has not expanded her areas of interest beyond the home often feels inadequate in social activities, particularly if she cannot join in the conversation in an informed manner.

It is also important to set a personal schedule for yourself. Care for your appearance, just as though you were preparing to go out into the "world of work" every day. Keeping yourself looking good for your own sake, for your husband, and for those you love should be even more important than putting on your best face for a more impersonal public world.

There are many things to do when you have the flexibility that accompanies being self-employed, so to speak, in your home. Christian women have the perfect opportunity to spend time reading and studying the Scriptures, praying and gathering for fellowship with other Christians. Those "at-home times" are great times for spiritual growth. As a Christian, I found reading and spending quiet time with the Lord a very important part of my life in those years spent working at home. Those quiet times are no less important to me today, just more difficult to set aside as I have less personal control of my time.

I also used some of my time at that season of my life to study painting for four years. And at the age of forty-three, I literally forced myself to learn to swim. That may sound like a small accomplishment to you, but as the original "chicken of the sea," it was a monumental hurdle for me. After I repeated the same course in beginning swimming three times at the "Y" in classes filled with little kids, I finally reached the point where I could swim, ultimately swimming a half-mile a day. That was a feeling of accomplishment!

Egged on by the voices of discontent within the secular world, some women today who are staying at home with their children are draining their energy feeling sorry for themselves. In the process of spending time on negative emotions, a very important season of life and the golden chances that they may never be able to recapture are lost. Self-pity is really self-centered and very selfish, in fact, one of the most crippling of emotions. As we turn in on ourselves, we miss all the people and opportunities around us—we miss life. We are incapacitated by a self-imposed affliction. We have walked into a "prison without bars" and locked the door behind ourselves. Jesus said He came to set the prisoners free. He can, if we will but let Him. We need to ask Him to release us from our prisons to become the persons He created us to be.

Whatever our role in life may be in the home, in the office, in the factory—wherever we live our lives—we are called to use our talents and our gifts to their fullest. God calls us to excellence.

God places within us a desire to excel. It is this that has urged Mary Crowley on over the years as she built that $400 million business. Mary describes it this way, "We have a 'Divine Discontent': a yearning, a drive to always do better."[1]

The building of relationships gives deeper meaning and influence to our lives. Women are so good at that. Generally, women are not content to live on the surface level with people, and that is one of our strong suits. Men often feel threatened if they must relate beneath the superficial level. In the development of relationships we are able to influence and meet needs in other hurting and lonely people—and the quality of our lives is increased in the process.

I want to share with you an example of how one woman uses her talents to reach out in a loving, compassionate way as she builds relationships with others who are hurting. Watching early morning television while traveling in Iowa one day, I saw a feature story about a big black and white, lovable character, very appropriately named Amanda the Panda, "The Bear with the Heart," the creation of a Des Moines, Iowa, woman who had decided to do what she could to minister to the needs of young children. I later went to visit this woman who had captured my imagination that morning. She was a delight. JoAnn Zimmerman, a mother of three, while working in the banking industry a few years ago, started thinking about the way children easily relate and open up to animal characters. With her own money she had a local theatrical shop design a seven-foot-tall, yet cuddly, panda bear suit for her, one with a big red heart on a ribbon around its neck.

As she visited schools, hospitals, and nursing homes in her costume, JoAnn discovered that the children she saw with the greatest needs were the ones who suffered from life-threatening illnesses and who were living at home. Often their visitors are infrequent. As JoAnn puts it, "Sometimes friends disappear fast for a child in this situation, and Amanda is faithful and loving."

She started specializing her efforts toward these children—and Amanda the Panda continued her visits to them, often until their deaths. There has never been any charge for those visits.

With her travels to see the children taking a great deal of time, JoAnn left her position with the bank. Her husband, Joe, took a second job to "support her habit," as JoAnn puts it. JoAnn's personal ministry has expanded to the point where she is now training other "Amandas," and her prayer is that there would be "Amandas" in cities all across the country. She has also been given assistance by a denominational social concerns council.

JoAnn's faith and prayer life are very vital to her. Her eyes glisten with tears as she tells of the simple faith of young children. The Lord, as He blesses others through her unique ministry, is also blessing her and her family. JoAnn says, "I think we have to make this world a better place in which to live. Whatever gifts we have been given are given by God to be shared with others. Can you imagine what a wonderful world it would be if everyone did that?"[2]

This is what one woman unselfishly did with her gifts. If you would meet JoAnn Zimmerman, a giver, and measure her attitude and obvious fulfillment against some who spend their lives demanding for themselves, there would be no doubt in your mind which approach to life works best. The world needs more JoAnn Zimmermans.

We may be the greatest lawyer, or housekeeper, or whatever, but are we the greatest person we can be? That's tougher to become, but it is really more important.

Developing our character is so extremely important, no matter where we spend our time or do our work. Our character will affect our work and all those with whom we have contact. It will affect them for good or ill. It was a wise person who said, "In the beginning, we make our habits. In the end, our habits make us." The circumstances of life, and sometimes people, can force situations upon us that we would not choose and do not like, but no thing or no one can force upon us the way in which we handle them.

The Bible teaches in 1 Thess. 5:23 that we humans are composed of three parts, body, soul (intellect, will, emotions), and spirit. Envision, if you will, three concentric circles, the innermost circle being our spirit, the middle circle our soul, and the outer circle our body. When we are "born again," we are born spiritually as the Spirit of God comes into our spirit and takes up residence within us. The Spirit of Jesus lives in us. How can it be explained? It can't. How it happens is a mystery, but happen it does.

A friend of mine recently went from lifelong church activity and belief in God into a personal relationship with Christ. As she put it, "I don't understand it, but since I asked Jesus into my heart, everything is different. The Bible makes sense to me—and I know He's real. It's just so different. *I'm* so different."

What we humans generally do is allow our body, motivated by our five senses, to determine our thoughts and actions. Sometimes our soul, our intellect, overrules the bodily desires of our senses, and we exercise our will power to override our human inclinations. What God wants is for our spirit, indwelled and controlled by His Spirit, to direct our soul and body. That is how He changes us from the inside out.

As He indwells us and we draw closer to Him and seek Him more, His thoughts become the thoughts we begin to think. As God's love indwells us, we are able to love even the unlovable with His love, for His love is the same for everyone, no matter what his or her condition.

Agapē, mentioned earlier, is the Greek word for that unconditional love of God. It is His *agapē* love that enables us to forgive our enemies as Jesus forgave those who nailed Him to the cross. You see, we start developing His character as He resides within us. That is not possible to do in a full and lasting manner by merely exercising our own will power.

As God starts to shape His character within us, we don't have to try to be like anyone else. If we allow Him to make us into what He created us to be, there is nothing more satisfying or rewarding. We usually set our own sights too low. God has great things in store for us.

You probably know that a keystone is the crucial building block placed at the crown, the uppermost top, of an arch. Perhaps you have seen the arch in St. Louis, which reaches high into the sky next to the Mississippi River on the waterfront of that

Midwestern city. Without its keystone, that arch would fall to the ground and crumble.

Jesus Christ is the keystone in our lives. He holds the pieces of our lives in place as we build them to the full height of our potential—toward Him and what He created us to become. We can build our lives on our own, if we choose. But without that vital keystone to hold together the building of our lives, it will not stand the test of time.

One day I was struck by the wide variety of ways in which God uses His women as they submit their lives to Him and make Him the keystone of building that life. Within a twenty-four-hour period I had the opportunity to meet and listen both to Miss America of 1980, and an eighty-three-year-old woman missionary to India.

The first, Cheryl Prewitt Blackwood, a beautiful, vivacious young woman in her early twenties, was visiting Washington, sharing her story with a group of senators' wives. She told how God had guided her life from childhood to the point of winning the crown in the Miss America contest. It seems that Cheryl had been in a terrible accident as a child, suffering many facial cuts and a crushed leg. Turning to the Lord in complete and simple trust over the years that followed, Cheryl saw God work miracles. Her face healed without noticeable scars. The doctors watched the progress by x-rays as a new bone was formed in her leg, like a cocoon of calcium. At one point after a prayer for healing, the leg, which was two inches shorter than the other, grew in a few seconds to perfectly match the other leg—a miracle she tells of wherever she speaks.

This remarkable woman, a singer, has taken her talent and her story all across the country. She had told her story of God's blessing to President Carter the day before. She shared with him how God had healed her and led her into the Miss America pageant. Her entire life was committed to serving her Lord, and He had honored her commitment.

The other woman was a frail little white-haired lady I heard at a church service. She told of her recent experience in the poverty-stricken nation of India. She had been a Christian missionary to India for many years and now at eighty-three she told how she was returning to work until God would call her home to heaven.

Not long before, she had fallen into a rain-swollen river. The river was rapidly moving and its waters were polluted and refuse-laden. The strong current carried this elderly woman, her bones brittle with age, miles and miles downstream. Though her mind was filled with thoughts of her imminent death, she was miraculously saved.

A man who was standing at the edge of the water had quickly reached out and grabbed her arm, pulling her uninjured to safety. She believes he was there by "divine appointment." Her wrinkled face broke into a smile as she said, "I thought sure it was my time and that the Father was taking me home, but He let me know that He isn't finished with me yet. So I'm going back to India." Now in the sunset years of her life, she was returning to serve her brothers and sisters in that far land as she allowed God's love to pour through her.

Here are two women, distinct and different, with individual talents and abilities, both serving the same God. I was struck with the diversity of our individual calls, yet I was deeply aware that we all share a common call to serve Christ—and to serve Him with excellence.

Consider the Men

There is enormous overlap between the sexes. Intelligence, talent, courage, ambition, nurturance, emotional vulnerability—all are human qualities that we share. If each sex brings to these qualities a different style and a special flavor, it can only make both of them richer.

Annie Gottlieb

A new member of the White House administrative staff was attending an in-house meeting being held in my office. I happened to be the only woman present. The four men and I were discussing some proposed legislation and how it would affect women. The new man, in conversation, used some term which, after having said it, he was afraid might have sounded "sexist." It obviously was innocuous, because I can't even recall what it was, and I had not noticed it at the time. He had, however, quickly apologized for his choice of words. Another man, an attorney friend with whom I had developed a good working relationship said, "Oh, that's all right. Dee's one of the guys."

Then as he realized how that sounded, he quickly added, "Dee, I'm sorry. I just meant that you aren't ultrasensitive."

Reassuring them both that everything was fine, I then suggested, "Let's forget all this and get to work." Whatever had been said had not caught my attention, and I considered it a compliment that my colleague thought of me as just an equal member of the staff, just another human being doing my job.

But I thought of that incident after the meeting concluded and the men had left my office. It was really too bad that these sensitive and well-intentioned male colleagues were uncomfortable and ill at ease with women in a professional situation. It made it difficult for all concerned just to get about the business at hand. The increasing sensitivity of men to the needs of women and to their own attitudes toward women was good. But wasn't this too much?

You may have heard a man say something like this, as I have: "You don't know whether to open a door for a woman anymore or let it swing shut in her face after you. If you hold the door open she may cuss you out and tell you she is perfectly capable of taking care of herself. If you let it slam in her face she may say, 'Where have chivalry and good manners gone?' You can't win!"

It is a dilemma. Just where do men fit into this modern-day equation? What have the women's liberation movement, the sexual revolution, and the eroding moral code in America done to American men? Or, rather, how are men responding? An entire volume could be written about that subject.

I discussed this subject over coffee one day with Steve, a successful young Washington businessman whom I knew to be fair-minded and objective. He and his contemporaries were on the front line in the professional arena, working with competent, capable women in job situations, in this city full of career women.

Steve said, "Men are really working much better with women in a professional setting now. They are usually very open to them and welcome them into the professional career roles."

I asked, "Are men really happy to have women there, Steve? Do they want them there?"

He responded, "Well, men don't want to be judged by society as being chauvinists or against equality. Sure, there are problems sometimes. It depends on the person, just as it does with men. But many men are bending over backwards for women just because they *are* women. And they think they have to appear to be fair-minded."

"Do you think it bothers some of the men at times—inside?" I pressed on.

"Oh, there's no doubt about it. Sometimes they promote or hire women, even though they're not qualified enough, and everyone is frustrated about it later in a working situation," he answered.

I appreciated Steve's candor. However, the relationships and attitudes of men toward women at work were only part of the human interaction between the sexes to be examined.

In the October 1983 issue of *McCall's,* an insightful article by Anne Gottlieb appeared in which she acknowledged that men and women don't appear as different from each other as they used to:

> How do we like the prospect of a unisex world? The majority of women seem to like it just fine . . . except for one nagging problem. And that is that men, mysteriously, have wilted.
>
> There's something missing, and it's something that both men and women miss: a special vibrancy, vitality, gusto, pride, that we once recognized as distinctively masculine.
>
> "Much is being said among American women today about the strange dearth of vital men," Betty Friedan wrote recently. "I go into a town to lecture, and I hear about all the wonderful, dynamic women who have emerged in every field in that town. But, frequently, they're flat, they complain they're tired."
>
> There is compelling evidence that what men need (much more than women, who seem to require less reassurance of their gender identity) is a clearly defined difference between the sexes. Every known human culture, until the late twentieth century, has provided such a difference, creating an elaborate and often quite arbitrary contrast between men's and women's activities, dress and behavior.

Gottlieb goes on to cite anthropologist Margaret Mead's classic work *Male and Female,* in which Mead points to the only biologically based constant difference between men's and women's roles in societies. Women have always had the role of child-bearing and giving the primary care to children. Beyond that, societies varied in many, and almost any, ways, except that, Mead wrote, "in every known human society, the male's need for achievement can be recognized. . . . Their maleness, in fact, has to be underwritten by preventing women from entering some field or performing some feat."

Continuing, Gottlieb writes, "It is this kind of exclusion of women that our society—quite rightly—no longer accepts. . . . We have finally begun to recognize the injustice to society, as well as to women, of barring women's talents from any field of human endeavor. We have not yet recognized the genuine needs of men that lay behind that exclusion—needs that, if we understand them, can perhaps be filled in a way that is not at women's expense."

As she examines the subject, Gottlieb lists three reasons that in her opinion cause men to need roles distinct from women. Again citing Mead, Gottlieb first notes the fact that baby boys have to separate themselves from their mothers in order to discover and develop their male identity. Gottlieb suggests that men need time to be together with just men to "replenish their sense of being men." Of course, women are most everywhere today so it is not an easy thing for men to find a place alone, without women.

Second, she points to the most obvious achievement of women that men cannot duplicate—having babies. Gottlieb says:

> He [the young male] needs to know that when *he* grows up he will be able to do something just as important that women *can't* do.
> Since this will have to be cultural, not biological, it is something he will have to *do*, rather than something he must merely wait for, as a girl waits to grow up and become a mother. Hence, the importance of *achievement* to men. It is, in a sense, all they have for self-definition. . . . If a woman can do everything a man can do *and* have babies, what use is a man?
> Fatherhood at its most involved is not the same as motherhood.

Third, the author cites the biological differences between men and women in their physical strength and the more aggressive nature of men, pointing out that this difference "most cultures have used as the raw material for a unique male role."

Margaret Mead is quoted as acknowledging that young men probably do have a need to physically prove themselves and that "in the past the hunt and warfare have provided the most common means of such validation."

Gottlieb reminds us that in modern society these are not the "honored" activities that they were in earlier societies. Hunting is often considered "exploitive of nature" and, with the threat of nuclear weaponry, the possibility of war is gravely threatening.

In summary, Gottlieb writes:

> Women can help by accepting men's need to be alone together at times and by respecting the father-son bond, even (or especially)

when divorce has divided the family. Dr. Richard C. Robertiello adds that "a man needs a woman who will affirm his masculine power, enjoy it, enhance it and get something from it, rather than envy it and try to destroy it."

Some of the classic expressions of male power can be integrated into the compassionate man of the '80s. . . . Apart from their sexual anatomy, greater muscular strength is men's unique human possession. If they are not allowed to use it in a particularly masculine form of nurture, they feel useless, emasculated, and vengeful.[1]

The next time you are out in a family restaurant notice the families as they eat their meal together. In the average situation, the children, and the husband, center on the mother—just as the home centers on her. The woman is the center, the heart, of the family. She draws everyone together in that family.

Now if the husband is stripped of any meaningful position in the family, and if the wife is also working, partially filling the provider's role, where does it leave that man? What is left but for him to flounder, like a little lost boy, or to rebel in some way—not sure just who he is, or what his purpose is?

Gottlieb suggested the protection of their loved ones from harm, sports, and healthy physical activities as some outlets for this need in men.

One example of male protection is described by Ann Dummet in an article in *New Blackfriars*, "Racism and Sexism: A False Analogy": "Male prejudice against women is often combined with respect for women. . . . The slogan 'Women and children first,' invoked in shipwreck and other disasters, is not an expression of contempt or hostility but of a belief in the special *importance* of women and children in the crucial moments when the choice of who among many are to deserve survival is a real one."[2]

Man was created and equipped to provide for and to protect his family—his wife and children. Woman was created to bear and nurture the children. Mere physical anatomy does demand recognition of that basic truth.

To be deluded or intimidated into denying those basic and obvious facts loses sight of logic and common sense. At the same time, these truths about the male and female genders should in no way be employed to impair or impede the development of our talents as individuals. Refusing to accept our inherent legacy of gender not only ignores truth; it results in a warped self-image and often a consuming anger and frustration.

In the frustration produced by hurts and injustices they have suffered, some women have, in essence, denied their womanhood in the pursuit of correction and retribution. Where truth is denied, confusion abounds. We can deny truth, but truth is still truth.

In addition to the changing social attitudes prompted by the women's liberation movement, men have had to cope with another confusing element in their self-image and identity search. This disruptive factor predated by several years the development of the women's movement initiated by the appearance of Friedan's *Feminine Mystique* and other influential books of the '60s. This was the "Playboy Mentality" which emerged in 1953 when Hugh Hefner's *Playboy* magazine made its debut.

An article by Barbara Ehrenreich in the June 1983 *Ms.* magazine discussed the effect of the "Playboy mentality" on men and on the family. She recalls that in the 1950s, when she was growing up, men were becoming increasingly open in their hostility toward marriage. Concerned psychiatrists analyzed this behavior as "flight from maturity," a rebellion against conformity and against the assumption of responsibility that accompanied the role of husband and father.

This attitude was fueled by Hugh Hefner's *Playboy* magazine, which began in 1953 and set about perpetuating the American mythic tradition that "women are the civilizers and entrappers; men the footloose adventurers." In the *Playboy* view, wives were simply out to take husbands for all they could get, while, if truth be known, they spent most of their time "relaxing, reading, watching TV, playing cards, socializing," and generally acting like gold-diggers. Why suffer the spirit-crushing imprisonment of marriage, *Playboy* asked, when life could be so pleasurable in a bachelor apartment complete with stereo, bar, and a limitless supply of Playboy bunnies? By 1956, according to Ms. Ehrenreich, there were nearly a million regular readers of this "manifesto of male revolt."[3]

Ms. Ehrenreich brought these facts as a defense against some of the charges leveled at the feminist movement. She believes these factors had kicked off an "anti-family" attitude and code of conduct among men, some time before the genesis of the feminist movement.

Her point has merit. A family friend has been a street minister on Times Square in New York City, bringing support to the broken lives and lost souls wandering there. He told me, "The 'Playboy mentality' hit men in the '50s, they lived it out in the '60s, and in the '70s and '80s they have been reaping the harvest in their children. The Bible says our sins will find us out." Observation of the "cause and effect" system in life proves it is true.

As the "Playboy mentality" grew over the years and gained acceptance from "sophisticated society," the demeaning and victimizing of women as sex objects increased. The "Playboy mentality" not only degrades women, but it also reduces men to their "private parts"; that becomes their identity and demeans them in the process. Advertising, entertainment, and the arts have all been affected. Our educational institutions, the media— all the institutions of public expression have been affected.

If we then couple the "Playboy mentality" with the extremes in the "liberation movement," should we wonder that our traditionally accepted Judeo-Christian moral code came under attack, and with it marriage and the family? And, for spice, throw into this social stew the advancements of mankind's ability and knowledge in the areas of science and technology, lulling many into the false assumption that God was outdated and obsolete. Therefore, the illogical "logical" assumption came about that mankind could handle rewriting the old traditional moral code which was now out of style. And of course, almost all who bought into that mindset wanted to write their own rules.

When we set aside God's laws, which bring harmony to our lives, the certain results are chaos and confusion. The attitude toward morals and life that advocates "If it feels good do it" has come to roost. We need to get back to realizing and teaching our children that self-indulgence will and does make us sick.

My friend Carson Daly put it well in a conversation we had on this subject: "If you are really feeling indulgent you might sit down and eat five pieces of gooey chocolate candy, but you wouldn't eat five pounds. At a certain point you're not enjoying it anymore. It is interesting in a curious way, the most sensual and the most positively enjoyable way of living your life is the most moral way. In the same way if you deprive yourself of always eating everything you want, of always going everywhere you want, if you exercise some self-control, you will enjoy things more. If you have that piece of chocolate cake once in awhile it will be wonderful, whereas, if you eat chocolate cake every day until it comes out of your ears, it is not going to mean very much."

Addressing this same issue, the Summer 1983 *American Educator* says:

> These traditional values—middle-class values if you will—are threatened today by a contempt for the pursuit of excellence and for loyalty, by the belief that rewards should be distributed regardless of effort, by the encouragement of self-expression and self-gratification rather than self-restraint, and by the definition of sexual activity as a kind of sport unrelated to lasting commitment and unrelated to childbearing and, therefore, acceptable in any form.[4]

In the building of character it is vital to develop self-control and self-denial, but in institutions of public expression these qualities are not presented as desirable options today. However, given any deliberative thought, we can see that the exercise of these personal qualities will lead to the most personally desirable results in our lives.

No matter where we may choose to place the blame for the societal problems we encounter today, the truth is that we get in trouble when we leave God out of the equation of our lives. And this holds whether we are women, men, or children.

It is very evident that if we were to live by the biblical instructions for our marriage and family relationships, men and women, as well as their children, would have those needs met that God placed within them. His instructions for right living are not just capricious whimsy; they are practical and fulfilling, when followed.

God designed the government of the family for the benefit of all. One of the best articles I have read about man's role as husband and father, lived as the Bible directs, was written by David R. Mains. It appeared in the March 1983 *Decision* magazine. Mains draws a parallel between job responsibilities and advancement into management within a company and a man's becoming the spiritual head of his family, as the Bible directs. When a man assumes the position of spiritual headship and administers it properly, identity and the need for self-identification are no longer problems. Mains writes:

> A promotion [at work] means that someone with authority has finally asked, "How would you like to be in charge here?"
>
> Spiritual headship in the family is a matter of promotion as well. God, who has the authority, is asking, "How would you like to be in charge here?" But while most men rise to the challenge of job advancement, they seem to be strangely defeated at the thought of spiritual management in the family. . . .
>
> Ephesians 5:23-24 reads, "For the husband is the head of the wife as Christ is the head of the church. . . . As the church is subject to Christ, so let wives also be subject in everything to their husbands."
>
> The same idea is recorded in 1 Corinthians 11:3: "I want you to understand that the head of every man is Christ, the head of a woman is her husband. . . ." This lends ego gratification for the male if he gives headship the supremacy meaning.
>
> Yet few of us, knowing even just a little about the nature of Christ, would hold that our Lord viewed the male sex to be supreme.
>
> Lording it over others was not Jesus' style of earthly leadership. An attitude of male supremacy was not detectable in any way in his relationship with women. Jesus' supremacy stems from his God nature, his being the Christ, not from his sex. . . .
>
> Male chauvinism and Biblical headship are miles apart. The first is anti-Christ, the second is Christlike. . . .
>
> In reality, the roles that husband and wife play in a marriage seem to be more a matter of agreement between married partners, a matter of the intricate meshing of personalities, a matter of preference in life-styles, than it is a matter of Biblical precept. Unfortunately, we often argue over the forms which are really extra-Biblical and these arguments serve as smokescreens to keep us from understanding the real issue of spiritual headship.
>
> Consequently, when I work with small groups of men, or in marital counseling situations, I attempt to focus first on the matter of the responsibility inherent with headship as contrasted to the roles of the sexes.
>
> Headship means that the husband assumes ultimate responsibility for the spiritual well-being of his family. . . .

> Unfortunately, many Christian men like the honor that goes with headship, but they are not enthused about the job description. . . .
> His example, what he models, who he is spiritually, is nine-tenths of the job!

Mains relates how he and his wife, as a management team in their home, frequently evaluate the quality of their marriage and the development of their family. He goes on to explain:

> In other words, I exercise my spiritual headship by inviting my wife to work alongside me to develop the spiritual climate of our home. Through the years we have become a team, joint-workers in this area. She assists me by helping me grow into my full development as a healthy, spiritual adult. . . . There is tremendous strength in a spiritual team working in concert.
> A question needs to be answered by Christian husbands and fathers. Someone very important has asked, "How would you like to be in charge here?"
> "Take the job!"[5]

What a tremendous insight into a very responsible and balanced view of a husband's spiritual headship in the government of the family. Some say that biblical headship does not apply today, that it was just for that earlier culture. While it is true that culture has changed since biblical times, human nature has not, nor has God's Word and His established order of authority. From one perspective, the husband is in a servant role to the wife; more accurately, they are serving each other.

Ephesians 5 goes on in verse 25 to *command* men to love their wives. It reads, "And you husbands, show the same kind of love to your wives as Christ showed to the church when He died for her."

David Mains not only obviously understands his responsibility for spiritual leadership, but also for fulfilling the biblical directive on how to relate to his wife. His wife, Karen Burton Mains, wrote a short companion article in the same publication. It speaks for itself, I believe, and I quote her comments in their entirety to provide her total perspective as a Christian wife living within God's proper family order.

> What does spiritual headship look like? We have problems fleshing out the spiritual because we cannot see it. We need form,

substance, a model, something to bump against, something to hold if the frustration unseen becomes real.

In our home spiritual leadership is tangible. It is seeable. It is pillows stacked on the living room sofa where someone prayed late last night. It is the back of a man in the study bending into the dim light. It is a Bible so used that the pages are soft, the binding malleable. It is a mind so disciplined that it struggles to consider all issues from God's perspective.

Spiritual headship is a man who loves worship, who calls a family together on Saturday evening to ready their hearts for tomorrow's praise. It is the reminder: "Come home early. Tomorrow is Sunday."

It is the familiar question we tease and joke about but would feel neglected if he never asked, "How are you doing spiritually?"

It is barging into a room and finding a husband and father on his knees. It is the crease marks on the forehead of a man after he has pressed it to the bed in prayer.

Spiritual headship is a husband who invites his wife to walk beside him in every area of his calling, a man who believes more strongly in her spiritual gifts than she herself does.

Spiritual headship is one-to-one accountability Bible study on Amos with the oldest teen-ager. It is bedtime with the ten-year-old and discussing the playmate who has changed his reading material from a pornographic magazine to Christian comics.

It is reading a story by Flannery O'Connor and laughing at her hilarious humanity and then discussing the action of Grace in the tale.

Spiritual headship is a man on Saturday, with the house full of wife, four children, two dogs, one pregnant cat, guests and extended family, desperately hunting for a quiet place for a time of prayer.

Spiritual headship is a man, sometimes exasperatingly human, who nevertheless gives the spiritual life tangible form.[6]

A wife could give her husband no greater tribute than to be able to write an article such as that about him.

Now that does not mean that the Mainses do not have problems in their home, because they are human. We all are, and therefore we all fail at times. However, it would be hard imagining that a husband and father would have an identity and self-esteem problem if he were taking to heart the biblical guidelines for the husband's position of spiritual authority in the home.

It would also be hard to imagine that a wife who was cared for and loved and brought in as such a vital partner in the marriage relationship would not feel fulfilled and valued. It is evident that God is the keystone in this family.

Unfortunately, in twentieth century America the authority figures who touch children's lives in their early years are almost exclusively women—teachers in their schools and Sunday schools, crossing guards at their schools, den mothers in their clubs, chaperones on their field trips, nurses in hospitals, clerks in supermarkets, salespeople in stores, and so on. Additionally, in many families the father neglects his responsibilities in the home and abdicates his authority in the children's lives to the mother. The children are left without a strong male influence in their young lives and are not exposed to a father who is a role model of parenting according to God's design. Many mothers today are faced with the challenge of filling the role of both mother and father, and in order to add balance in the lives of their children must seek outside male influence for them.

I am only sorry that Roger and I did not have a close personal walk and commitment to Christ when our children were young. Reading the Mainses' articles, one can easily see the powerful impact this kind of strong Christian influence in the home would have upon children and the life benefits they would reap from it.

Some women are afraid that having the husband in spiritual authority places the wife's welfare in jeopardy in some way. However, when a husband properly fills his position, there is no reason for concern. If he should abuse his position of spiritual authority he will sacrifice in respect what he may gain through a wife's obedience. A dominant man is a lonely man. "Rulership" is a perversion of headship.

In order for marriage to succeed, it has to be "worked at." Men must "will" to love their wives, and women must "will" to submit to their husbands. It is only through a free commitment of the will that a good marriage relationship will take place on a lasting and consistent basis and not be controlled by exterior circumstances or sheer emotion.

There is responsibility in spiritual authority: it is a protective covering for the wife. The biblical marriage relationship might be compared to a fine Swiss clock, the woman representing the delicate, fragile, important inner works and the man the protective cover.

In the Winter 1979 issue of *Human Life Review*, Michael Novak wrote:

> Society has a special stake in the development of married family life. Without strong, enlightened, spiritually nourishing families, the future of society looks bleak indeed. The family is the original, and still the most effective, department of health, education, and welfare. If it fails to teach honesty, courage, a desire for excellence, and a whole host of basic skills, it is exceedingly difficult for any other agency to make up for its failures.[7]

In the rest of my conversation with my friend Steve, whom I mentioned earlier, we discussed his family—his wife of a year and a half and their brand-new baby. That Steve loves his family was evident as he told me of his views on family from a personal perspective.

Steve, a committed Christian, said, "Men are losing sight of what it means to be a husband and a father. We have lost our cultural heritage that our parents and grandparents had. They knew how to raise children. In today's culture it is hard to see children the way the psalmist saw them, as a blessing from the Lord. Men friends say, 'Boy, will you be tied down when you get married! It will change your lifestyle completely.' No one is telling us about the fact that our families are special and a blessing to us."

As we discussed today's social attitudes, Steve noted, "Our culture pushes men to be heroes at the office, and doesn't acknowledge that it is a virtue to spend time with your family. It makes denying responsibility easier. The church could be of great help if it would focus on the importance of being a father who is the spiritual leader in the home, and one who appreciates his wife and her role as mother. The church should have a greater impact on our culture, and not the other way around."

As we discussed the church, Steve said, "I sense a despair among some of the clergy about their inability to turn people around. This leads them to think that there is no point in teaching that which their congregations may not want to hear. In fact, that is exactly what needs to be taught. But, people need a life-

changing experience with Christ before they can truly hear what
the church should be saying."

We continually come back to the same point—that unless
Christ is the keystone of our building, we build in vain. If women
have a distorted idea of their identity and position within a
marriage, there is trouble. If men have a distorted view of their
responsibility and position, there is trouble.

Strange how women, becoming more aggressive, may push
men, and if the men topple, then the women lose respect for
them. If women do not allow men to be whole, they are denying
themselves whole men. Men and women need each other. That
is God's design.

Society, reflecting the "Playboy mentality" and the lack of
commitment to others, degrades true feeling and elevates false
feelings. Love is presented as a sensuous emotion that uses others
rather than as a deep commitment that serves the needs and
interests of others, subordinating one's own self-interests. As
men have succumbed to these false feelings, they have suffered
the after-effects also.

Carson Daly expressed it this way: "One of the things I noticed
about the young men is that they have many, many things that
never come to the surface. They don't even talk about them
to their best friends. They don't talk about them to their mothers
and they don't have wives. Lots of them have things they are
ashamed of and feel guilty about. They have been living according to the 'new morality.' It is sad, for the only way they can
express their guilt or talk about it at all is maybe in the locker
room. Of course, that is the antithesis of repentance and an
amendment of their lives. It is exactly the opposite of what
they need. They need forgiveness and healing. In their hearts
they know what they have done is wrong. They need their ideas
and attitudes about women healed. They need Christ."

Many men, as well as women, need a healing of attitudes.
Society needs some changed attitudes also. For example, many
urge men to allow themselves to be free enough to show their
emotions. And Carson is right. Men don't show their feelings
or speak of their inner thoughts often. That is not healthy. Usually they have been conditioned by our culture to think it is a
sign of weakness to show or admit to emotion. "Macho men"

don't do that, society teaches. If being a "macho man" in the eyes of society is the basis of your identity as a man, revealing your sensitivity can be very threatening.

But, consider how society responds. I recall how former Senator Ed Muskie suffered a grave political setback in his bid for the presidency when he was televised with a tear in his eye and a catch in his throat, as he defended his wife, the woman he loved, who had been unjustly criticized and was hurt. Why was that act judged to be a sign of weakness and a crack in his veneer of strength, when, in fact, his deep feeling of concern for his wife should have been lauded and applauded? For is it not a virtue to have a compassionate, caring heart? It is a *strong* man who does not feel his manhood threatened by showing tenderness. Why are we so quick to jump on each other's visible humanity and cry "weakness"? We are all human.

Carson summed up her thought by saying, "I think our society needs healing on such a large scale, it is unbelievable. So many of us need forgiveness and need to forgive others of so many things."

Men and women need to acknowledge that they are equal, but that they are different. There are some today who actually have lost sight of that fact. I had one woman tell me that outside of the capability of having children, women and men were the same, that every other difference is learned. She was not only ignoring the facts but seemed to be indicating that to be different from men was to be inferior in some way. Her sentiments are a by-product of societal attitudes toward women in recent years. These attitudes need correcting and, more important, healing.

In the September 1981 *Reader's Digest,* an article entitled "Male/Female: The *Other* Difference" pointed out some researched differences.

Men and women *are* different—obviously so in size, anatomy and sexual function. But some scientists now believe that they are unlike in more fundamental ways. Men and women seem to *experience* the world differently, not merely because of the ways they were brought up in it, but because they feel it with a different sensitivity of touch, hear it with different aural responses, puzzle out its problems with different cells in their brains. . . .

Many scientists are now convinced that hormones "imprint" sexuality on the brains of a large number of animal species by changing the nerve-cell structure. But what about humans? So far, the best evidence is indirect. For years researchers have known that men's and women's mental functions are organized somewhat differently. Men appear to have more "laterality"—that is, their functions are separately controlled by the left or right hemisphere of the brain, while women's seem diffused through both hemispheres. . . . Women usually mature earlier than men, which means that their hemispheric processes may have less time to draw apart. They retain more nerve-transmission mechanisms in the connective tissue between the two hemispheres and may thus be better able to coordinate the efforts of both hemispheres. Men generally do better in activities where the two hemispheres don't compete with, and thus hamper, each other.[8]

Communication is the key to understanding. As an example, before men can meet the needs of their wives, they have to know what those needs are. Therefore, they need to listen to their wives. Women are more verbal, generally, and have a great desire, as well as a greater ability, to communicate their feelings, needs, and thoughts. Husbands often give women "things," when what women want more than anything else is their husbands' attention.

Some men only know how to relate to women as lovers or as children. That creates many of the wrong attitudes men have toward women. The "Playboy mentality" has taken its toll on society and has contributed heavily to wrong attitudes. True maturity in Christ can correct these and other distorted attitudes.

Men also need to realize that since they choose their own mates, to treat them with less than respect is really an indictment of their own judgment. It is an exciting thing to have another human being commit the rest of his or her life to you. That honor should be celebrated by both the husband and the wife. We need to appreciate each other. In homes where God's order is observed, the needed maturing process is underway.

A line from "Wedding Song," heard at many of today's marriage ceremonies, says it very well. "Woman draws her life from man and gives it back again." In the very beginning, God created woman by drawing her from Adam's side, and she freely gave

herself back to him. The song goes on, "And there is love."*
The free giving of oneself to another is the greatest gift. To
accept each other, with appreciation, is God's desire and design.

Whether married or single, both men and women share the
same need for identity, a solution to life's struggles and the
key to direction and purpose in life. All those things are to be
found in a daily relationship with the living God.

Women:
The Key to the Future

Next to God we are indebted to women,
first for life itself, and then
for making it worth living.

Christian Nestell Bovee

In this book I have talked of many things. The message I have endeavored to convey has formed and grown within me to such an extent that I felt a great need—not just a desire, but a need—to express it.

As I have watched and listened to all the clamor and confusion about women and their concerns, the charges and countercharges, the hurts and injustices that have festered into rage and hostility, a cry has come forth from the center of my being, begging to be heard. I want to exclaim, "Stop! There's more. You're missing the most important part of the problem. Women have a deep hunger inside. And what you are offering will only bring temporary satisfaction and won't meet women's deepest needs. While you are focusing on the lesser, the greater beggars for an audience. All the while the world hungers for something that women have the capability and opportunity to bring to it. Oh, please, listen—for women are the 'pearl of great price' in today's society. Their value is far beyond dollars. They have a high calling. Don't drown out that call in a sea of conflicting, confusing voices."

As you read what I have written, you may have wondered that I have appeared to marry the sacred and the secular, the material and the spiritual. I have indeed. To discuss only the secular, material side of life when discussing human beings, women or men, is like considering only the shell and not the oyster, for that which is of the most value is that which is inside. To treat the problems otherwise is to behave like a physician who keeps wiping away blood without finding the wound and stitching it closed to heal.

The foolishness of ignoring the spiritual while focusing on the natural, or material, is addressed in the best-seller *The Secret Kingdom* by Pat Robertson. In the opening segment of the book, the crisis and chaos which is growing in every segment of life worldwide is addressed. In analyzing current world attitudes, Robertson quoted the late Francis A. Schaeffer, the Christian philosopher-theologian, from his book *A Christian Manifesto:*

> They [the humanists, believers in man rather than God] have reduced Man to even less than his natural finiteness by seeing him only as a complex arrangement of molecules, made complex by blind chance. Instead of seeing him as something great who is significant even in his sinning, they see Man in his essence only as an intrinsically competitive animal, that has no other basic operating principle than natural selection brought about by the strongest, the fittest, ending on top. And they see Man as acting in his way both individually and collectively as society.[1]

Returning to the words of *The Secret Kingdom*, we hear this message:

> Fortunately, a Voice speaks steadily and clearly into the turmoil and dread of the day, a Voice that contradicts our finitude and limitation and restriction. It says, "But seek first His kingdom and His righteousness; and all these things shall be added to you."
> Obviously the words are those of Jesus, climaxing a teaching about food, clothing, shelter, and all the "things" needed for life. . . .
> His point immediately established a fact that the world has in large measure refused to consider—the fact that an invisible world undergirds, surrounds, and interpenetrates the visible world in which we live. Indeed, it controls the visible world, for it is unrestricted, unlimited, infinite.[2]

In the New Testament story, Nicodemus, a ruler among the Jews, came to Jesus one night and spoke to Him. He told Jesus he knew He must be from God because of all the things He could do.
Robertson writes:

> The Lord skipped all the small talk and went to the heart of Nicodemus' concern, preserving for all generations an understand-

ing of the indispensable initial step toward life in an invisible world that governs all else. The kingdom of God is not really a place—at least not yet—but rather a state of being in which men, women, and children have yielded all sovereignty to the one and only true sovereign, Almighty God. It is the rule of God in the hearts, minds, and wills of people—the state in which the unlimited power and blessing of the unlimited Lord are forthcoming.

The natural eye cannot see this domain, and Jesus quickly explained that. He probably spoke softly, but distinctly. ". . . unless one is born again, he cannot *see* the kingdom of God. . . ."

God is spirit. Those who would know Him—who would worship Him—must do so in spirit. . . . Flesh begets flesh and spirit begets spirit, so this rebirth must be accomplished by God the Holy Spirit. . . .

The kingdom of heaven is based on an invisible, spiritual reality, capable of visible effects.

This is the reality the world craves so badly.[3]

I believe that to be true. And when it comes to the deepest issues of life we should be united by a shared spiritual bond. It doesn't matter if my political beliefs are not the same as yours. It doesn't matter whether we are women or we are men, for our spiritual kinship transcends all our various differences that can bring division. Indeed, so many elements in today's society bring division that unless there is a transcending power and purpose that unites us all, we will remain fragmented.

Some in the feminist movement and some in the countermovement are often found in two emotionally charged camps glaring at each other. A contest based upon contempt is not a solution to the problems of today's women. Other *women* are not the enemy, and *men* are not the enemy. *Distortion of truth* is the enemy. The real truth is to be found in the person and the teachings of the One who is truth, Jesus Christ.

Women need to build up other women, not tear them down, playing "I gotcha." This seems to be the popular game of the day—to go on the attack whenever another stumbles, even slightly.

"I gotcha" seems to have become a favorite pastime with many, especially some in the media, who pursue it with great ardor. Perhaps the "Watergate era" was its genesis, when investigative reporting and exposure of wrongdoing was ushered in as the mode of the journalistic day. Though most members of the press across the country are hard-working and seek to be fair and objective, some who have national impact seem to be caught up in this critical approach to their profession. Certainly it is true that we need honest, thorough, and objective reporting. However, for our individual and corporate health, don't we as a nation and as a people need a dose of the positive—an antidote for the negative and necessary acknowledgment of our problems and our failures?

An irony has developed. Imperfect journalists are seeking perfection in imperfect people in public life (past as well as present) in an imperfect world. A similar national public mindset is thus encouraged. Then when the *inevitable* imperfections are found, great cries of dismay and condemnation go up—even when errors are unintended, slight, or merely products of journalistic speculation.

Stranger yet is the fact that many members of the national media, according to a great percentage of their own poll responses, profess to hold no belief in the restraints of moral absolutes, rights and wrongs, but apparently consider the Judeo-Christian code of ethics and moral behavior as antiquated and obsolete. One is led to wonder, against what moral yardstick do these journalists measure the actions of others to judge their moral failures? If we expect to find *any* perfect people anywhere, we will be sadly disappointed. *There are none.*

We will find no perfect Christians either, for try as we may, we are not able to lead perfect lives. Better and changed lives, yes, but there will be times when we will fail. We are not perfect. It is a frustrating fact, but true nonetheless. An ongoing commitment to strive for perfection is the key to Christian living.

As a Christian, I always feel uncomfortable and inadequate, under heavy responsibility, whenever I sense that people admire me unduly, for one reason or another. I know how very human I am and I don't want to disappoint them. I want them to quickly shift their attention to Jesus, the only perfect example for us all. He is the one for Christians to pattern their lives upon.

And, please, let's not lose our sense of humor. It seems that so many are so easily offended today. This is true of many modern women. We need to take life seriously, but not take ourselves too seriously. When we do the latter, we are not at ease with life and we intimidate others, making them uncomfortable in our presence. The atmosphere surrounding us becomes so charged and supersensitive that no one acts naturally, even if he tries. We need to laugh—yes, even sometimes at ourselves.

A perceptive observer of history and human relationships once observed, "You can't change a nation without changing her women."

Sadly, the ability, the worth, the value, the influence, the contributions of women down through history have often been overlooked or slighted. Only solitary voices have sounded forth here and there to proclaim the greatness of women.

Those who have expressed their appreciation of women have done so in a variety of forms. A sampling follows.

"Without women the beginnings of our life would be helpless; the middle devoid of pleasure; and the end, of consolation" (Victor Jouy, *Maxims*).

"Women control not the economy of the marketplace but the economy of eros; the life force in our society and our lives. What happens on our social surfaces, determining the level of happiness, energy, creativity, and solidarity in the nation. These values are primary in any society. When they deteriorate, all the king's horses and all the king's men cannot put them back together again" (George Gilder, *Sexual Suicide*).

"Disguise our bondage as we will, 'Tis woman, woman rules us still" (Thomas Moore, *Sovereign Woman*).

"Next to God himself, we are indebted to women—first for life itself and next for making it worth living" (Christian Nestell Bovee, *Thoughts, Feelings and Fancies*).

"Women. Their love inspires the poet, and their praise is his best reward—I don't think they are the first to see one's defects, but they are the first to catch the fragrance and the colour of a true poem. Fit the same intellect to a man and it is a bow-string, to a woman and it's a harp-string. She is vibratile and resonant all over, so she stirs with slighter musical tremblings of the air about her" (Oliver Wendell Holmes, *The Autocrat of the Breakfast-Table*).

"Have they not duties to fulfill—duties which are fundamental in all human life? Is it not women who ruin or sustain their homes, who regulate every detail of domestic life and therefore decide

what touches the human race most nearly? That is why they affect
most closely the good or bad habits of practically all mankind"
(François Fenelon, *The Education of Girls*, 1687).

An observation was made about the impact of women on
all of society by one of the men instrumental in the governmental
formation of the United States. John Adams, second president
of the United States, said, "From all that I had read of history
and government of human life and manners, I had drawn this
conclusion, that the manners of women were the most infallible
barometer, to ascertain the degree of morality and virtue of a
nation. . . . The Jews, the Greeks, the Romans, the Swiss, the
Dutch, all lost their public spirit and their republican forms of
government, when they lost the modesty and domestic virtues
of their women."[4]

In a tribute that still rings down through the years come the
words of the often-quoted French philosopher Alexis de Tocqueville, who traveled and studied our country to unearth her secrets
of success. In *Democracy in America*, de Tocqueville wrote, "And
now that I come near the end of this book in which I have
recorded so many considerable achievements of the Americans,
if anyone asks me what I think the chief cause of the extraordinary prosperity and growing power of this nation, I should answer that *it is due to the superiority of their women.*"[5]

The women of this country *are* special. *Women* are special.
We do bring a quality to life which cannot be duplicated by
men. Society needs us and men need us. Women can be the
key to our future.

This is true for many reasons. Women bring special qualities
to life, for they seem able to reflect God's character more clearly
with greater ease. While men are the spiritual head of the home,
women are the heart. Men have hardened themselves over the
years to face things of the world, as they have tried to provide
for and protect their families.

And, of course, there are many things for which we women
should feel a debt of gratitude to men. How often have we
stopped to consider that thousands upon thousands of men have
given their lives over the years to obtain and maintain the freedom we all enjoy in this country? There are some women today
who decry the fact that women are not slated for combat in

the military, but I can't recall hearing companion discussions in appreciation of the fact that men have served in the military, protecting our country and our lives ever since this country was founded.

Men and women need to appreciate each other. Midge Decter, in the February 6, 1983, *Washington Times,* writes:

> We Americans have many public disagreements, but privately it can be said that we are nowadays firmly bound together by a common unease. Something is going wrong with the constitution of our individual lives. Women, for instance, are noisily embattled, while men smolder in resentful silence. . . .
>
> How is it that a people blessed by God, or if you will, fate, with better health, longer lives, greater comfort and personal freedom and economic well-being than any previous peoples in history, should give so much evidence of deep trouble?[6]

Decter goes on to recount the many moral irresponsibilities and resultant problems of today's society. Her article is entitled "Why not discriminate in favor of the family?" The influence and responsibilities of parents and the home are cited as crucial to our society.

It is in the family that we learn to love, to serve, to exercise self-restraint. In the family the threads are chosen which are woven into the moral code of our social fabric. The family is the vital support system to the individual.

And it is in the homes of this nation that women are vitally needed, as the character of our young is shaped and molded. Even if the husband and father is in his proper role as the spiritual head of the home, the mother's role is crucial. It is crucial whether she works in the home full-time or works outside the home as well. The character of our nation is formed in her homes. Women truly have "the hand that rocks the world."

Women have an even more important role than just the physical care of their children. Jane Hansen, president of Women's Aglow Fellowship, writes:

> Her sorrow, her labor and travail are not completed (after natural childbirth) until she has birthed that one into the kingdom of God.
>
> God has written within the nature of woman, married or single,

the knowledge of what it is to labor and travail to bring forth life. I believe this applies to the spiritual as well as the physical.

In a unique way, a woman carries a burden for her family and loved ones. God has made her sensitive not only to the physical but to the emotional and spiritual needs of those around her.[7]

It is this spiritual influence of women that is the greatest need in our society today. Women have the ability to shape the face of this nation. But that work starts within each and every one of us and works out from there through our character, through our actions, through our influence, in both the spiritual realm and the natural.

Incorporating many facets of life in this work, I have addressed both timely facts and timeless truths. It has not been possible to produce a deep exhaustive work in any one area. Those readers who find a hunger, or even a flicker of interest, for searching beyond the surface of life, those who have an interest in a daily walk with Jesus Christ, I would encourage to look further. Ask Him to come into your heart. Read the works of other Christian authors—perhaps some I have quoted. Read the Bible, find other Christians, find a church. I can promise you it will be the best decision you have ever made and you will be embarking on the greatest adventure life has to offer. Some will doubt and some will scoff, I know. But think about it. You have everything to gain if it's real—and nothing to lose if it isn't. Truth doesn't have to be defended, only tried.

But, remember, God has no grandchildren. You don't come into the kingdom just because your mother or father was a Christian. It is not an automatic thing. There are no "of course" Christians. It requires a conscious decision, an act of free will, to accept Christ as Savior and Lord, and a deep tenderness toward God. In Colossians 2:10, we are told, ". . . in Him you have been made complete. . . ." We may try to be complete in other things, but this will work only for a while, if at all, and does not last. The key is to find out what it means to be "joint heirs with Christ" (Rom. 8:17).

To come into a walk with Christ takes commitment, a lasting commitment. And commitment, of any kind, seems to be out of vogue today. But if you make a commitment to Christ you will never be sorry, for you will find that the joy He brings is far beyond the temporary thrills of the world. You will discover that His blessedness is greater than mere happiness. The things of this world, upon which you will no longer center your life are nothing when compared to "eternal life" which you will receive in Christ.

A Christian friend said to me, "We all have mortal bodies, but we have immortal souls. And every person with whom we interact is either an immortal horror or an everlasting splendor." The decisions we make determine which we are—where we will spend eternity.

As you start upon your Christian journey through this life, you can never tell where it may take you. Looking back on my own life, I can recall as a young girl of about eleven lying one day on the living room floor of our modest little farmhouse and telling "that God, who was way off there someplace," I wanted to be a "saint." I had just read the life of a saint which had touched my young heart. I remember saying, "God, I would like to be a saint, but I don't know how. And I don't think I could—but I would like to."

I know now that a saint is simply a forgiven sinner, and I qualify on both counts. God heard that simple childlike prayer— and He answered it many years later. Little did I know then that my life path would lead from that little farm and the nearby one-room schoolhouse to Washington, D.C., and a position in the White House. God has been very gracious to me.

There is so much God wants to do with each one of us—far beyond our own imaginations. For you, it may never be anything as public as the route my life has taken, but it will be *just as important,* even if it doesn't take you out of your own neighborhood.

Jane Hansen writes in *Aglow* magazine:

> I believe that from the beginning God's purpose for the woman has been tremendous. His desire is that we would first of all allow Him to work in our own lives, letting Him make the necessary adjustments in us instead of our asking God to make adjustments in others' lives for our comfort or happiness. As we are turned, adjusted, we then become useful and effectual in His hand.
>
> The call to women today is to come and join forces with God. . . .

God is looking today for those who will give themselves to opposing those things that oppose Him, for calling forth (through faithful prayer) things that are not as though they were (Hebrews 11:1–3), that His plan and purpose might be fulfilled in the earth.[8]

We can move the hand of God in prayer. God opposes evil. Just as the Spirit of God is an ever-present force for good in the world, there are evil forces at work as well. It is common today to hear natural disasters called "acts of God." This is a misnomer. God's "perfect will" is for no evil or destructive things to occur. However, we live in a fallen world, imperfect and sinful. That is the cause for the evil of life. God *allows*, but never *causes* evil to befall us.

Another wrong impression that is often voiced is that "religion causes war." No. Man, not religion, causes war. Man may use a religious excuse to initiate war or violence, but *man* bears the guilt for destructive aggression. True Christianity, applied to life, is a relationship with Jesus Christ, who is love. That relationship is *based upon love*, Christ's love for us, our love for Him, and His love, through us, for our brothers and sisters. Anything less is a distortion of *true* Christianity. If everybody were to live a life transformed to the image of Christ, there would be no war, nor the need to defend ourselves against aggressors. Unfortunately, that requires a perfect world, and this is far from it. This is a sinful world.

Revolutionary things happen when true Christianity comes into our lives and the Lord's love starts reshaping our character.

> Love transforms—
> Ambition into aspiration,
> Greed into gratitude,
> Selfishness into service,
> Getting into giving,
> Demands into dedication.[9]

Christ calls upon us to serve our generation. That's not an easy call in an age of comfort, not conviction; an age of moral pollution, where drugs, alcohol, and promiscuity are used as "coping devices" just to get through life; an age where our possessions actually "possess" us; an age of accommodation where we employ tricks of conscience to justify our misdeeds, our sin.

In a recent newspaper I noticed a letter to the editor that put it well. It made the point that the intelligentsia of this age seem to feel that acknowledging a just and holy God will result in condemnation. So they tell themselves that there is no God, thus avoiding potential judgment and escaping into a false security as they continue to follow their own situational ethics.

To accommodate our own sin we are prone, very conveniently, to run our actions through *our own* moral grid, instead of God's laws. Thus we stand in judgment of Him, instead of realizing and acknowledging that He, in fact, stands in judgment of us.

Chuck Colson, in his book *Loving God*, cites Karl Menninger's startling book *Whatever Became of Sin?* as posing the most timely question anyone could ask of the church today. Colson writes, "The answer lies within each of us, but to find it we must come face to face with who we really are. This is a difficult process. That hidden self is buried deep inside our hearts, and, as Jeremiah warned, the human heart is deceitful above all things. Confronting that true self is an excruciating discovery, as I learned in prison after my conversion."[10]

I believe, along with Jane Hansen, that God has a special, high calling for today's women. The question is, are we willing to answer that call? Will we set our goals upon serving God and seeking His righteousness, which has eternal value, or upon seeking the things of this world, which will all pass away? It is our free choice.

God is touching His women today. This is a strategic time in human history and He has placed each one of us here. We are here by divine appointment, not by accident of nature.

Not only is this a strategic time; it is also a dangerous time. There is danger in our complacency. The next generation, and far more, depends upon the decisions made by women today. God is calling for women who are willing to stand in commitment, sacrificial commitment; women who are willing to stand in conviction, not counting the cost; women who will stand for His righteousness, even when it isn't easy. Senator Mark Hatfield once told me, at a time when I was under attack for my Christian stand, "Dee, remember, the wind is always strongest at the top of the mountain."

It is easy to do the comfortable things, but God is calling us to do things which are uncomfortable—to do them with courage. Ridicule and social scorn are very powerful deterrents to taking a stand for righteousness. Today's society gives little resistance to moral decline. But we do not have to accept as inevitable continuing social and moral decay.

We shouldn't set our sights on failure—rather we should hold up a high standard and strive to attain it.

God is calling His women to "stand in the gap" (Ezek. 22:30), to stand with Him, in face of the world's opposition; to stand in love, not condemnation—but to stand, nonetheless.

God may use you in surprising ways for He wants more for you than you want for yourself. God elevates. It will be the most exciting, rewarding way you could live your life.

François Fenelon wrote, "All virtue consists in having a willing heart. God will lead you by the hand, if only you do not doubt, and are filled with love for Him rather than fear for yourself."

A "willing heart" is the key. Are we willing to be obedient to the God of the universe?

What if, two thousand years ago, that young teen-aged girl named Mary had looked at the circumstances instead of heeding the call of God with a willing heart?

Have you ever thought about what she faced? Have you thought about her quiet courage, as well as the significance of her decision to say, "Yes, Lord. I want what You want for me"?

Mary was a young engaged but unmarried girl. To her friends and neighbors she appeared to be an unwed mother-to-be, in a day when that was very unacceptable. When she did marry, her husband was a poor, simple carpenter. They had to make a grueling trip by donkey to a far city, when she was very pregnant and, undoubtedly, very uncomfortable.

They were turned away from the local inn and put up in a barn full of animals. There, unattended in the hay, she had her baby—far from help, her mother, and the home she had so recently left.

For their child's safety, she and Joseph had to flee to Egypt, a long and arduous desert trip. There they were aliens in a foreign land. When they returned to Nazareth, they lived in an unfortunate part of the country, nowheresville. And always there was the lurking thought that Mary pondered in her heart, "This child is different. He has a greatness, but he will suffer in some strange way, and so will I."

Whenever we feel sorry for ourselves and are moved to complain, we need to think of the courage of that brave young girl who was used by God to reshape the course of the history of all creation. We should then take heart.

As God calls us to raise His banner of righteousness, He calls us to change the course of our country's future. We are called to stand, without embarrassment or apology, to face intimidation without being intimidated. America's women represent the last hope for restoring moral values in our society. As women are coming to a greater fullness in the use of their talents today, we need to come to a greater spiritual fullness as well.

The eighteenth century poet and historian Matthew Arnold wrote, "If ever the world sees a time when women shall come together purely and simply for the benefit and good of mankind, it will be a power such as the world has never seen."

I pray that the world will see that time in these present days.

Women might ask themselves the same question today that was posed to Queen Esther by her cousin Mordecai over twenty-five hundred years ago. Timing and circumstances presented the opportunity for Esther, a Jew, to intercede with King Ahasuerus on behalf of the Jewish nation. Though her very life hung in the balance, Esther did intercede, saving the Jewish people. She did so after her cousin asked, "And who knows but what you have come to the kingdom for such a time as this?" (Esth. 4:14).

Women have the opportunity to be used as a force for good in "such a time as this." God's timing is perfect—and our time is now. He has placed us in history at a time of great spiritual hunger. *Women* can be the ones to introduce to the Prince of Peace those whose souls hunger. *Women* can be God's peacemakers, rather than simply settling for being power-seekers.

There is so much more. *There is something far beyond equal rights. Let us seek the best.*

To be used of God requires that we come into relationship with Him, that we come to know Him. That requires spending time with Him, time in prayer communicating with Him. The power of prayer is the greatest power there is, yet it is the least recognized and developed resource available to modern humanity. Read about any of the great culture-changing revivals; ask the Billy Grahams and the Dr. Paul Chos of the evangelical world today about the power of prayer. They have personally experienced what a key it is.

There has never been a great move of God which was not undergirded with prayer. And women are the world's finest prayer warriors. If today's women will intercede, God will respond. Women can change their homes, their communities, their country and their world through their prayers. The ministry of intercession, interceding with God on behalf of other people and causes, is of great importance and impact.

Mary, Queen of Scotland, said, "I fear John Knox's prayers more than any army of ten thousand."

Women have been gifted with a greater sensitivity to spiritual things. Women are often the ones who respond to the Lord's call most quickly. This is for a number of reasons, I believe. Our culture seems to expect men to be tough-minded, implying that to be spiritual is a sign of weakness. Men have also been caught up in the busyness of the work place, often setting spiritual things aside because they were not placed high on their priority list.

As women have become involved in the marketplace in greater numbers, they, too, have lost some of their quiet time, such important time—time not only to talk to God, but to listen for that "still small voice" (1 Kings 19:12). We must not allow the rush and distractions of a busy life to consume us, to cost us that key opportunity to pursue the things of the spirit in the quietness of our hearts. We must place that time on the top of our list of priorities. We will never be sorry. We must heed the words, "Be still, and know that I am God" (Ps. 46:10, NKJV).

François Fenelon cautioned, "How can you expect God to speak to you in that gentle and inward voice which melts the soul, when you are making so much noise with your rapid reflections? Be silent, and God will speak again."

We need to retreat in order to advance. After spending quiet time with the Lord, which in the eyes of the world appears unproductive, we find that we go forth better equipped to deal with the things of the world. It is one of the many paradoxes, contradictions, in the Lord's spiritual kingdom. Dr. Robert H. Schuller, speaking on "The Hour of Power" television program, said that the cross was the greatest of contradictions. There God combined in a creative way both justice and mercy. The Bible tells us that we must lose our life to gain it (Luke 9:24). We have to die to this worldly life, let go of it by an act of the will, in order to gain spiritual, or eternal, life. A beautiful truth, yet a paradox. God's ways are not our ways (Isa. 55:8).

As I close this book, my deepest prayer is that I may have clothed my thoughts with the rights words to communicate to women even a fraction of the deep love God has for them, and how fervently He desires to use them to speak His peace to their generation, the peace which only He can bring to the hearts of each and every one of us. I believe God has a special mission for "His women."

Not long ago, I was listening to a tape of a sermon by Jack Van Impe on the death of Jesus. The tape was called "The Greatest Love Story Ever Told." As I pondered the agonizing events of the suffering and death of Jesus for our sins, a thought occurred to me—that men were the ones who inflicted the physical abuse and torture upon Jesus. In fact, the only woman directly involved in the entire incident was Pilate's wife, who interceded with her husband on behalf of Jesus. She had a dream about Jesus and told Pilate, when he was sitting in judgment of Jesus, to have nothing to do with this righteous man. But her warning was to no avail (Matt. 27:19).

It was men who scourged, mocked, and spat upon Jesus, who made Him carry the cross, crucified Him and laughed while they gambled for His clothes. I also realized that as far as I can find, there are no recorded incidences of women failing Jesus.

My point is not that women are better than men. Of course not; we are all sinners. Perhaps women's sins are sometimes just more subtle than men's. The point is, rather, that women are distinctly different from men, and uniquely equipped to carry out God's mission for today.

If women were to deny their special qualities, their true gifts as women, trying to model themselves after men, all of society would be distorted. Sensitive, loyal, faithful, brave, committed women willing to be used of God to speak His truth boldly would be sadly absent.

The events of human history do not unfold without God's notice. In our society today, for many of the reasons reviewed earlier in this book, we women are center stage. The spotlight of public attention is upon us. The question is, now what are we going to do with it? I believe, from the ranks of those women who are willing to serve Him, God is assembling a mighty army of women—women who will serve God and their generation, women who will introduce those seeking identity, fulfillment, purpose, and peace to that Prince of Peace, the True Liberator: Jesus Christ.

I have a friend named Jennifer who told me about a simple little lady called Nanny, her grandmother. Nanny loved the Lord and lived her life for Him. And she reflected His character. Nanny's family and friends all loved her. She made the hard times easier—and she and her loved ones lived through some hard times, times of real poverty. But they always seemed to have enough, not only for themselves, but to share with others. For you see, if Nanny had two jars of preserves she would give one away to someone who didn't have any. The Lord saw to it that her family always had enough—never very much—but enough.

Nanny lived to a vigorous old age; then, taking ill, she was confined to bed. When that day came the Lord had appointed for Nanny to come home to Him, she sat straight up and exclaimed, "Oh, I hear the most beautiful music!" And she smiled, as a peace and joy flooded her countenance.

Now the history books won't contain stories about Nanny. She wasn't rich and famous. But she served God and those around her in the special way for which He called her. Her life was a *true* success and, living in their memories, she still influences those who knew her. I am sure God ushered her home, greeting her with those words that would make all of life worthwhile, "Well done, my good and faithful servant" (Luke 19:17).

Proverbs 25:11 (NASB) says, "Like apples of gold in settings of silver is a word spoken in right circumstances." God has a "word in season" for today's world. Let us speak it.

Let us seek Him and the unique purpose for which He calls each one of us. Then let us call others to Him, where they will find personhood and peace in today's confusing world. And some day, we too will be greeted by our heavenly Father with those welcoming words "Well done."

Notes

Chapter 1

1. *Washington Post,* August 21, 1983.
2. *Washington Post,* June 30, 1983.

Chapter 2

1. *Typeline,* November 1982, vol. 15, no. 10, p. 1, Washington, D.C.: U.S. Government Printing Office.
2. *Ladies' Home Journal,* January 1984, p. 63.
3. *Glamour,* July 1983, p. 30.
4. Joanna L. Stratton, *Pioneer Women: Voices from the Kansas Frontier* (New York: Simon and Schuster, 1981), p. 79.
5. Ibid., p. 12.
6. Letter of Abigail Adams to John Adams in *Adams Family Correspondence,* L. H. Butterfield, ed., 4 vols. (Cambridge, Mass.: Harvard University Press, 1961), 1:369.

Chapter 3

1. Quoted in *Growing Strong in the Seasons of Life* by Charles R. Swindoll (Portland, Ore.: Multnomah Press, 1983), p. 138.
2. *The Review of the News,* December 3, 1980, p. 53.
3. *Washington Post,* April 27, 1971, p. 83.
4. Betty Friedan, *The Feminine Mystique* (New York: W. W. Norton, 1963), p. 77.
5. *America Today,* October 3, 1983, p. 4.
6. National Federation for Decency, P.O. Box 2440, Tupelo, MS 38803.
7. "Women: The Real Victims of Pornography," *Catholic Twin Circle,* October 30, 1983, p. 14.
8. Statistics supplied to the National Federation for Decency by Dr. Shirley O'Brien, University of Arizona.
9. Quoted in *The Affairs of Women,* by Colin Bingham (Milson's Point, New South Wales, Australia: Currawong Publishing Co., 1969), p. 97.
10. U.S. Department of Labor, Bureau of Labor Statistics, January 6, 1984.
11. Friedan, *Feminine Mystique,* p. 357.

Chapter 4

1. *Washington Times,* August 15, 1983, p. C1.
2. Phyllis Schlafly, *The Power of the Christian Woman* (Cincinnati: Standard Publishing, 1981), p. 15.
3. Ibid., p. 17.
4. Connaught C. Marshner, "The New Traditional Woman" (Free Congress Research and Education Foundation, 1982).
5. "Women vs. Women: Report from the Front Lines," *Glamour,* January 1984, p. 144.

Chapter 5

1. *Random House College Dictionary,* rev. ed. 1980, pp. 1312; 474.
2. Betty Friedan, *The Second Stage* (New York: Simon and Schuster, Summit Books, 1981), pp. 15–16.
3. Susan Bolotin, "Voices from the Post-Feminist Generation," *New York Times Magazine,* October 17, 1982, p. 31.
4. Carson Daly, "The Feminist in the Family: the Femme Fatale?," *Fidelity,* vol. 2, no. 6 (May 1983), p. 13.
5. *Los Angeles Times,* September 15, 1982, p. A1; *Washington Post,* January 1, 1984, p. H1; *New York Times,* February 7, 1983, sec. B.
6. *Ms.* Magazine, February 1981.
7. Article by Robert J. Samuelson, *Washington Post,* July 19, 1983, p. D7.
8. Judy Linscott, "Differing Views on Women's Road to Corporate Success," *Des Moines Register,* January 1984.
9. Quoted in *Her Name Is Woman* by Gien Karssen (Colorado Springs: NavPress, 1975), p. 77.
10. Jane E. Brody, "Divorce's Stress Exacts Long-Term Health Toll," *New York Times,* December 13, 1983, p. C5.
11. Linscott, "Differing Views."
12. Anne Taylor Fleming, "Women, Success and Cruelty," CBS-Radio's "Spectrum," 1983.
13. "Essays on Feminism versus Feminine," *The Phyllis Schlafly Report,* vol. 16, no. 5, sec. 1 (December 1982).
14. Anita Shreve, "Careers and the Lure of Motherhood," *New York Times Magazine,* November 21, 1982, p. 38.
15. Maureen Dowd, "Many Women in Poll Equate Values of Job and Family Life," *New York Times,* December 4, 1983, p. 1.

Chapter 6

1. "Resolved: Women Have It at Least As Good As Men, Part II," *Firing Line,* November 30, 1982, p. 26. Copyright 1983, the Southern Educational Communications Association, P.O. Box 5966, Columbia, S.C. 29250. Complete transcripts are available for $3.00 each.
2. *Confessions,* bk. 1, ch. 1, trans. by Watts.

Chapter 7
   1. John 4:42, TLB.
   2. James F. Kennedy, *Why I Believe* (Waco, Tex.: Word Books, 1980), p. 125.
   3. Mary C. Crowley, *Be Somebody: God Doesn't Take Time to Make a Nobody* (Irving, Tex.: Crescendo Book Publications, 1974), p. 31.

Chapter 8
   1. Mary Crowley, *Be Somebody.*
   2. Dale Hanson Bourke, "The Winning Ways of Mary Crowley," *Today's Christian Woman,* Summer 1983, p. 47.
   3. *Christianity Today,* February 4, 1983, p. 56.
   4. George W. Cornell, "Noted Women Believe Prayer Made Difference During Crises," October 2, 1982.
   5. *Random House College Dictionary,* p. 1143.
   6. "We Have a Gender Gap in Our Friendships, Too," *USA Today,* August 23, 1983.
   7. Kay Holmquist, "The Woman at the Helm of TWU," *The Pioneer,* Winter 1981, p. 12.

Chapter 9
   1. Malcolm Muggeridge, *The Wealth of Families: Ethics and Economics in the 1980s* (Washington, D.C.: The American Family Institute, 1982), p. 113.
   2. *Monthly Vital Statistic Report,* National Center for Health Statistics, vol. 32, no. 12 (March 26, 1984), p. 1.
   3. *Focus on the Family Newsletter,* March 1984, p. 12.
   4. "Twenty-Four Hours in the Religious and Spiritual Life of America," a poll conducted by the George Gallup Organization, Inc., April 1984, Summary of Key Findings.
   5. Spencer Rich, "Family Census: Traditional Households Are Still the Norm," *Washington Post,* November 19, 1982.
   6. Pearl Sydenstricker Buck, *To My Daughters, With Love* (New York: John Day Co., 1967), pp. 184–86.
   7. Matt. 25:15–30.
   8. Sandi Frantzen, "The Biblical Woman: Let's Free Her to Serve," *Moody Monthly,* February 1983, pp. 9–10.
   9. Darrell Sifford, "Church Should Counsel Gays, Ex-Priest Says," *Miami Herald,* November 27, 1983.
   10. *USA Today,* August 10, 1983, p. 9A.
   11. Judy Mann, "Working," *Washington Post,* June 29, 1983.
   12. Dr. James Dobson, *Dr. Dobson Answers Your Questions* (Wheaton, Ill.: Tyndale House Publishers, 1983), pp. 26–27.

13. *The Quotable Woman*, 1800–1981, comp. and ed. Elaine Partnow (New York: Facts on File, Inc., 1977, 1982), p. 75.

14. Deborah Fallows, "Why Mothers Should Stay Home," *Washington Monthly*, January 1982, p. 53.

15. Gladys Seashore, *The New Me* (Minneapolis: His International Service, 1972), p. 35.

16. Lee Michael Katz, "Hard Choice: More Moms Make Kids Their Careers," *USA Today*, February 2, 1983, p. 3D.

Chapter 10

1. Charles R. Swindoll, *Growing Strong in the Seasons of Life*, p. 13.

2. *The Faith of Helen Keller* (Kansas City, Mo.: Hallmark Editions, Hallmark Cards, Inc., 1967), p. 24.

3. Barbara J. Burrow, "That Woman Is a Success . . ." (Kansas City, Mo.: Hallmark Cards, Inc.) © 1979, Hallmark Cards, Inc., reprinted by permission.

Chapter 11

1. "We 'Liberated' Mothers Aren't," *Washington Post*, February 5, 1984, p. D1.

2. Christopher Tietze, *Induced Abortion: A World Review* (New York: Population Council in New York, 1983), p. 33.

3. *Life Report*, January 19, 1984, p. 4.

4. Francis A. Schaeffer and C. Everett Koop, M.D., *Whatever Happened to the Human Race?* (Old Tappan, N.J.: Fleming H. Revell Co., 1979), p. 40.

5. Ibid.

6. Dr. Bart T. Heffernan, "Diary of Every Man," *Debate: The People's Diary* (Fort Lauderdale, Fla.: Debate, Inc.), pp. 18–19.

7. Bernard Nathanson and Richard Ostling, *Aborting America* (New York: Pinnacle Books, 1981), pref.

8. Bernard N. Nathanson, M.D., and Adelle Nathanson, *The Abortion Papers: Inside the Abortion Mentality*, quoted in *Life Report*, January 1984.

9. Jean Staker Garton, *Who Broke the Baby?* (Minneapolis: Bethany Fellowship, 1979), p. 7.

10. Ibid., pp. 9–10.

11. Ibid., p. 15.

12. See n. 3.

13. T. Noonan, Jr., "The Experience of Pain by the Unborn," *Human Life Review*, Fall 1981, vol. 7, no. 4, pp. 7–19. Reprinted from *New Perspectives on Human Abortions* (Frederick, Md.: University Publications of America, Aletha Books, 1981).

14. Norman Fost, David Chudwin, and Daniel Wikler, "The Limited

Moral Significance of Fetal Viability," Hastings Center *Report*, December 1980, pp. 12–13.

15. Center for Documenting the American Holocaust, 1982. P.O. Box 99, Palm Springs, CA 92263.

16. AP news release, Richard Carelli, June 15, 1983, Washington, D.C.

17. Mother Theresa of Calcutta, *The Love of Christ*, ed. Georges Gorrée and Jean Barbier (San Francisco: Harper and Row, 1980), pp. 38–39.

18. Schlafly, *The Power of the Christian Woman*, p. 54.

19. *Whatever Happened to the Human Race?*, pp. 41–43.

20. Ronald Reagan, "Abortion and the Conscience of a Nation," *Human Life Review*, Spring 1983.

21. *Washington Post*, May 21, 1983.

22. Abortion: Judicial and Legislative Control, Issue Brief No. IB74019, Congressional Research Service, Library of Congress, updated January 10, 1984.

23. *New York Times*, February 15, 1984, pp. B1, B4.

24. Dr. Jeffrey L. Lenow, "The Fetus as a Patient: Emerging Rights as a Person?," *The American Journal of Law and Medicine*, vol. 9, no. 1 (Spring 1983), p. 2.

25. Dr. Peter Singer, "Sanctity of Life or Quality of Life?," *Pediatrics*, vol. 72, no. 1 (July 1983), p. 129.

26. Nancyjo Mann, *Washington Times*, August 3, 1983, p. C3.

Chapter 12

1. Rosalie Mills Appleby, *Herbert Hoover* (Nashville: Thomas Nelson Publishers, 1978), unnumbered page in section titled "God's Everything—Jesus Christ."

2. Ibid.

3. Quoted in *Her Name Is Woman* by Gien Karssen (Colorado Springs: NavPress, 1975), bk. 1, p. 173.

4. Ibid., p. 168.

5. Ibid., p. 171.

6. Excerpts from interviews reported in *Moody Monthly*, February 1983: Ruth Senter, p. 14; Elisabeth Elliot, pp. 12–13; Bruce Waltke, p. 13; Howard Hendricks, p. 11. Statement by Iverna Tompkins in *Ministries* Magazine, Winter 1983–84, p. 41.

7. "Is Feminism Biblical?" *Charisma*, January 1984, p. 9.

8. Iverna Tompkins, *The Worth of a Woman* (Plainfield, NJ: Logos, 1978), p. 119.

Chapter 13

1. *Mary Crowley: A Celebration—The First, The Tenth, The Fifteenth . . . Twenty-Five Years* (Dallas: Home Interiors & Gifts, Inc., 1983).

2. *Our Sunday Visitor*, September 18, 1983, pp. 4–5.

Chapter 14

1. Annie Gottlieb, "What Men Need from Women," *McCall's,* October 1983; condensed in *Reader's Digest,* January 1984.

2. Ann Dummet, "Racism and Sexism: A False Analogy," *New Blackfriars* 56 (November 1975):484, 490.

3. Barbara Ehrenreich, "The 'Playboy' Man and the American Family," *Ms.* Magazine, June 1983, p. 14.

4. *American Educator,* Summer 1983, p. 9.

5. David R. Mains, "Who's in Charge Here?," *Decision,* March 1983, pp. 6, 7.

6. Karen Burton Mains, "What Does Spiritual Headship Mean?," *Decision,* March 1983, p. 6.

7. Michael Novak, "Men without Women," *Human Life Review,* Winter 1979, p. 63.

8. "Male/Female: The Other Difference," *Newsweek,* May 18, 1981; reprinted in *Reader's Digest,* September 1981, pp. 129–32; used by permission of *Newsweek.*

Chapter 15

1. Quoted in *The Secret Kingdom* by Pat Robertson (Nashville: Thomas Nelson Publishers, 1982), p. 32.

2. Robertson, *The Secret Kingdom,* pp. 35–36.

3. Ibid., pp. 48–50.

4. John Quincy Adams, quoted in *Attack on the Family* by James Robison (Wheaton, Ill.: Tyndale House Publishers, 1981), p. 33.

5. Alexis de Tocqueville, *Democracy in America,* trans. George Lawrence (1835, reprint, Garden City, N.Y.: Doubleday, Anchor Books, 1969), p. 603.

6. Midge Decter, "Why Not Discriminate in Favor of the Family?," *Washington Times,* February 6, 1983, p. C1. Reprinted from "For the Family," by Midge Decter, from *Policy Review,* Issue No. 27 (Winter 1984). *Policy Review* is a publication of The Heritage Foundation, 214 Massachusetts Avenue, N.E., Washington, D.C. 20002.

7. Jane Hansen, "Aglow . . . A Mighty Tool in God's Hand," *Aglow* Magazine, September/October 1982, p. 3.

8. Ibid.

9. Mary Crowley, *Be Somebody,* p. 23.

10. Charles Colson, *Loving God* (Grand Rapids: Zondervan, 1983), p. 97.

Acknowledgments

For the use of quotations not acknowledged elsewhere in this book, the author expresses her gratitude. These quotations are from:

"Viewpoint" by Mary E. Stoltz, in *Glamour* magazine, July 1983, used by courtesy of the author.

Pioneer Women: Voices from the Kansas Frontier by Joanna L. Stratton, by courtesy of Simon and Schuster.

The Power of the Christian Woman by Phyllis Schlafly, by courtesy of Standard Publishing Company and the author.

"The New Traditional Woman" by Connaught C. Marshner, by courtesy of the author.

The Second Stage by Betty Friedan, by courtesy of Simon and Schuster.

"Voices from the Post-Feminist Generation," by Susan Bolotin, copyright © 1982 by the New York Times Company. Reprinted by permission.

"The Feminist in the Family: the Femme Fatale?" by Carson Daly, by courtesy of the author.

"Essays on Feminism versus Feminine" by Phyllis Schlafly, excerpted from *The Phyllis Schlafly Report*, used by courtesy of Eagle Trust Fund.

"The Winning Ways of Mary Crowley" by Dale Hanson Bourke, excerpted from *Today's Christian Woman* and used by Courtesy of *Today's Christian Woman*.

To My Daughters With Love by Pearl S. Buck (The John Day Co.) Copyright © 1967 by The Pearl S. Buck Foundation, Inc. Reprinted by permission of Harper & Row, Publishers, Inc.

"The Biblical Woman: Let's Free Her to Serve" by Sandi Frantzen, excerpted from *Moody Monthly*, February 1983, and used by courtesy of the author.

Dr. Dobson Answers Your Questions by James Dobson, published by Tyndale House Publishers, Inc., © 1982 by James Dobson. Used by permission.

Who Broke the Baby? by Jean Staker Garton, copyright 1979 Bethany Fellowship, Inc., used by courtesy of Bethany House Publishers.

Washington Times, August 3, 1983, statements of Nancyjo Mann by her kind permission.

Mary Crowley: A Celebration—The First, The Tenth, The Fifteenth . . . Twenty-Five Years, by courtesy of Home Interiors & Gifts, Inc.

"What Men Need from Women" by Annie Gottlieb, excerpted from *McCall's* magazine, October 1983, used by courtesy of the author.

"Who's in Charge Here?," © 1982 by David R. Mains, and "What Does Spiritual Headship Mean?," © 1982 by Karen Burton Mains, excerpted from *Decision* magazine, March 1983, and used by courtesy of the authors.

The Secret Kingdom by Pat Robertson, by courtesy of Thomas Nelson Publishers.

"Aglow . . . A Mighty Tool in God's Hand" by Jane Hansen, excerpted from *Aglow* magazine, September/October 1982, by courtesy of the author.

DEE JEPSEN, former Special Assistant to the President for Public Liaison to women's organizations, is the wife of U.S. Senator Roger Jepsen, the senior senator from Iowa, and actively assists him in his senatorial duties as well as his political campaigns. An articulate and inspirational speaker, she offers a voice for all American women, including those who are uncomfortable with the more extreme ideologies of either feminist or traditional movements. She has been a frequent guest on local and nationally syndicated radio and television programs and featured in numerous magazine articles, in addition to addressing a wide variety of audiences around the country. She was born on an Iowa farm, educated in a one-room country school, and assisted with the care of her younger brother at age thirteen, when her mother died. She was a founding owner of a successful small business; she is also a talented painter and has been active in women's theater productions. Senator and Mrs. Jepsen are parents of six grown children and have five grandchildren. They make their home in the Davenport, Iowa, area and in Alexandria, Virginia.